christ in a post-christian world

CHrist in a
post-christian
world

**How can we believe in Jesus Christ
when those around us
believe differently
—or not at all?**

pamela Dickey young

**Fortress Press
Minneapolis**

CHRIST IN A POST-CHRISTIAN WORLD

Biblical quotations unless otherwise noted are from the New Revised Standard Version Bible, copyright © 1989 by the Division of Christian Education of the National Council of the Churches of Christ in the United States of America. Used by permission.

Excerpt from Alice Walker's *The Color Purple* copyright © 1982 Harcourt Brace, San Diego. Used by permission of the publisher.

Cover illustration: *Welcome to the Water Planet,* by James Rosenquist, 1987, 14-1/2" x13-3/16", collage on paper, collection of the artist. Copyright © 1995 James Rosenquist/Licensed by VAGA, New York, NY. Used by permission.

Author photo: Sparks Studio
Cover and text design: Joseph Bonyata

Library of Congress Cataloging-in-Publication Data

Young, Pamela Dickey, 1955-
    Christ in a post-Christian world : how can we believe in Jesus
    Christ when those around us believe differently—or not at all?
    / Pamela Dickey Young
        p.   cm.
    Includes bibliographical references and index.
    ISBN 0-8006-2915-9 (alk. paper)
    1. Religious pluralism—Christianity 2. Christianity and other
religions. 3. Feminist theology. I. Title
BR 127.Y5 1995
261.2—dc20   95-20439
                                                         CIP

The paper used in this publication meets the minimum requirements of American National Standard for Information Sciences—Permanence of Paper for Printed Library Materials, ANSI Z329.4–1984.

Manufactured in the U.S.A.   AF–1-2915

99   98   97   96   95   1   2   3   4   5   6   7   8   9   10

Contents

92281

vi

Preface

Many people in previous times assumed that we simply inherited our ways of being religious from our parents and communities. Today we are conscious that, despite our religious inheritances, we have to choose for ourselves whether to adopt the religious stances of the families into which we are born, whether to adopt some other tradition, or whether to let religion play any meaningful part in our lives at all. Such choice is all the more important when we survey the world around us and see the diversity of ways of being religious available immediately at hand. The choice of a religious tradition and particular ways of following it are especially significant for women, who have often experienced themselves as constricted and oppressed by inherited traditions. We need to make our religious choices conscious of the human search for authenticity and conscious of the fact that not all ways of being religious offer the same possibilities for authenticity and integrity. Sometimes we wrongly assume that specific religious traditions are monolithic, that all ways of being Christian, for example, are the same. To adhere to a religious tradition does not necessarily mean to accept uncritically a whole program of thoughts, beliefs, and actions.

In this book I struggle with the question of religious identity by exploring the possibility of a Christianity that does not subordinate women or claim necessary superiority over those of other religious traditions or no tradition. This book represents the intersection of many theological questions that have been pressing themselves on me for the last few years. Most of my work has been focused on the question of intersecting identities and the problems and possibilities posed by those identities. What does it mean to see oneself as feminist and Christian at the same time? What does it mean to claim a particular religious identity in the late twentieth century? What does continued adherence to the Christian tradition mean in a world where, on the one hand, Christianity has too often been allied with the power of empire and where, on the other, we can and ought no longer to assume the privileges of such imperial alliances? What does a feminist have to say about Christian imperialism? Can one begin to formulate a Christian theology that is neither imperialistic nor patriarchal? How do we claim our own communal and individual identities at the nexus of a diverse set of adjectival descriptors, and how do we help others to understand those identities? How shall we use such terms as "feminist" and "Christian" to describe ourselves and our communities to others who would not see themselves in these terms? Can one privilege particularity, the specific details of very diverse religious outlooks and very different life experiences, without losing sight of possible general claims?

These questions are of interest to the wide variety of people for whom issues of religious identity are pressing ones. Although the subject matter of this book requires philosophical and theological argumentation and a certain measure of detail, I hope that it will also be accessible to and appeal to the reader whose interest in the questions is at least as much existential as academic, one who is seeking to clarify her or his own religious identity in the late twentieth century.

I argue that understanding oneself and one's life in terms of the Christian symbol system need not entail either imperialism (Christian superiority) or patriarchy and, indeed, that the specificity of Christian tradition is *one possible entrée* into the broad questions of truth, goodness, and beauty in a world of competing claims.

A book is always the culmination of a long process, and there are many people without whose support this project would not have been possible. I received a Theological Scholarship and Research Award from the Association of Theological Schools in the United States and Canada in 1992-93, which supplemented my sabbatical salary. This award,

viii

aimed at younger scholars, included, in addition to supplementary funding, funding to meet with a mentor, someone who would discuss the project in process. It was in this way that I came to know Dr. Anne Carr from the Divinity School at the University of Chicago. Anne is a wonderful and generous conversation partner and her support, commentary, and friendship have been crucial to the completion of this book. I am indebted to the Association of Theological Schools in the United States and Canada for their financial support and for supporting the brilliant idea that scholars seeking to establish themselves should look to more established scholars in developing their research profiles. I am also grateful to my colleagues at Queen's Theological College and Queen's University for the uninter-   ix
rupted sabbatical time to work on this book and for their continued interest in my work, and to my students, who are continually pushing me to clarify my thoughts.

I want to thank John Badertscher of the University of Winnipeg for commenting that the aesthetic dimension was lacking in my Presidential Address to the Canadian Theological Society in 1992. This pushed me to explore the place of aesthetics in theology.

Parts of this book were presented as the Belk Lecture at Wesleyan College in Macon, Georgia, in 1991 and at Vancouver School of Theology in 1992.

I am grateful to the many friends who have supported my academic writing. I have been particularly struck this year by the powerful and empowering friendships of many women who, whether they have been directly interested in theology or not, have given me the energy to bring this book to completion.

Finally, I want to thank Jerry Roddy and Linda Thomas for help at various stages along the way and especially to thank Linda for her help with the index, Fortress Press for its continued support of my work, and editors Michael West and Joe Bonyata for their helpfulness and good advice.

1
Introduction:
Beyond Christian
Imperialism and Patriarchy

Posing the Questions, Viewing the Contexts

Since its very beginnings Christianity has had to reckon with the fact that it is only one religious tradition among many in the world. Today, however, the world religious context is such that one of the most pressing issues in Christian theology is to formulate theological approaches to the plurality of world religious traditions.

Until very recently the principal (although certainly not the only) way in which Christians related to those of other religious traditions was to see them as objects of missionizing people whose eternal salvation depended on their conversion to Christianity. Although this point of view is still officially the stance of many of the more conservative Christian churches and is unofficially held by many in the more mainline churches, most mainline denominations have begun to rethink their views of other religious traditions.

This rethinking occurs for a variety of reasons. The main reason is simply that most of us do not live in the "splendid isolation" we once did. Instead of hearing about Hinduism from a missionary back from India, our next-door neighbors are Hindus. Muslims are building a mosque across the parking lot from the church. A brother-in-law is Jewish. We have to rethink our notions that Canada or the United States are "Christian" countries. The Hindus and Muslims and Jews and

Buddhists we know are good people. They adhere to their religious traditions as well or better than we who profess to be Christian adhere to ours. They have no desire to be Christians and we have to ask ourselves if, in all conscience, we think they would somehow be better people if they converted to Christianity. In the light of such recognition, churches began to realize that their traditional stances toward Jews, Muslims, Hindus, Buddhists, and so on, might not suffice for life in the "global village."

Too, there are many who are looking to nontraditional religious options such as Wicca or other goddess traditions or the variety of New Age religious possibilities. And there are many more who see any way of being religious as an expendable option. Christians must be able to understand and explain their own choices when faced with the host of other available ways of being human, both religious and not specifically religious.

Many in the churches have also come to realize that when Christian churches were engaged in converting others to Christianity, the Christian message often came aided and abetted by foreign governments who wished to control the people and resources of a particular area. Thus, whether missionaries intended it or not, Christianity was the religion of conquerors, and was often used to further the imperialistic aims of certain governments. Intertwining the message of Jesus Christ as only, sole, and sufficient savior with the aims of empires has often led to Christianity's being seen by non-Christians as itself necessarily and without remainder imperialistic. Jews experienced the Holocaust as the ultimate horrific act of Christian anti-Semitism. Christians have been pushed to rethink the Christian message and how it has been taught and lived because members of other faith groups have begun to articulate that their only experience of Christianity has been as an instrument of domination and control, torture and death.

Another cluster of issues arising within the Christian tradition itself forces a rethinking. Many Christians have begun to ask if the God of love that they know through the witness of the Bible and through Jesus Christ is really the kind of God who would limit God's love to the (relatively speaking) few human beings who called themselves Christians. What can and should Christians claim about God's love and grace and salvation? This question gives rise to numerous others about the authority and interpretation of the Bible, about what claims can and should be made for Jesus Christ, about the church's role in salvation, and so on.

Many Christian theologians are uneasy about the imperialistic claims Christians have often made for their own tradition and the implications those claims have had for Christian attitudes toward and relationships with other religious traditions. So they are seeking alternative ways to understand and make Christian claims.

Options after Christian Imperialism

The current discussion of Christian stances toward the plurality of world religions tends to focus on three main positions, usually labeled "exclusivist," "inclusivist," and "pluralist." Exclusivists, inclusivists, and pluralists, although their arguments take a variety of forms, all seek to answer the question: can religious traditions other than Christianity be said to offer salvation, or, alternatively put, can they be said to be true or to contain truth?

The exclusivist position is the one that most Christians have traditionally espoused. Those who hold such a position maintain that there is no salvation apart from God's salvation of humanity in Jesus Christ; and unless one knows and accepts Jesus as unique, sole, and sufficient savior, one cannot be saved. Thus the salvation of human beings depends on the Christian gospel being preached throughout the whole world, offering people the possibility of hearing the gospel and explicitly accepting the salvation offered in Jesus.[1]

Inclusivists bring together an understanding of God's working for salvation through all the world's religions with claims about the uniqueness and finality of God's revelation in Jesus Christ. Other religious traditions can be evaluated positively insofar as God's grace, fully manifest in Jesus Christ, can be discerned as working through them. They offer salvation only insofar as the grace constitutively offered in Jesus Christ is operative through them. Therefore, they offer partial truths.[2]

Pluralists maintain that religious traditions other than Christianity also offer salvation, a salvation not derivative from Christianity.[3] Therefore Christians should withhold "judgments of relative value between Christianity and other ways."[4]

Knowledge of God (or of ultimate reality) is partial in Christianity as it is elsewhere. All religious responses are incomplete. Pluralists evaluate other religious traditions positively. There is no one true religion; there are many, often because the notion of "truth" is seen entirely as truth relative to a given context. Truth is contextually relative either because there is no one reality but many or because reality is one, but on account of the faultiness of human perception we perceive and image it in irreducibly and incomparably multiple ways.

Exclusivists are often regarded as triumphalist or imperialist because they claim that they alone have access to God's grace and God's truth. They are also often seen as putting limits on the love or grace of God that they say they seek to communicate. Conversely, exclusivists might argue that neither inclusivism nor pluralism comes to terms with the particularity of Christianity, with its very specific and definite views of God and Jesus Christ.[5]

Inclusivists are also often accused of triumphalism or imperialism because they assume the truth and salvific value of Christianity is normative and they evaluate all other religious traditions from this untested assumption. Inclusivists regard the incarnation of God in Jesus as God's crucial and final revelation, central to human history. They safeguard the integrity of the Christian tradition at the price of a view of human history that seems, at least on the face of it, to devalue the integrity of other traditions.

Pluralists, on the other hand, tend either to compromise the integrity of the Christian tradition by playing down its central symbols in favor of more "universal" or "generic" central symbols (e.g., Hick's Eternal One)[6] or to compromise Christianity's (or any other religious tradition's) ability to state the truth by claiming that its truth, like all other truths, is simply relative to its context.[7]

A Feminist Option

Within religious traditions generally, and in Christianity in particular, are many feminists who are uneasy about the way patriarchy and Christianity have been so closely intertwined. In a patriarchal view of the world maleness is the normative way of being human and femaleness is seen as secondary and derivative. The assumption of normative maleness has led to social structures that foster male dominance and female subordination and to theoretical justifications for such social structures (including theological justifications). Because I accept the legitimacy of the project of feminist criticism, the Christian theological position that I formulate here is also a feminist theological position. In the next chapter I will explore some of the resources feminism has to offer to the project at hand.

Much of the writing that has been done on the plurality of world religions focuses on interreligious dialogue, and a large portion of it is by Christian theologians seeking to enter into such dialogues. My aim, slightly different from most of these, is to outline a Christian theology, focusing in particular on the understanding of Christ (christology), that might serve theologians well as they seek to think through the Christian tradition in light of the claims made on Christianity by other religious traditions and by feminism. I seek a Christian theology that is neither imperialistic nor patriarchal.

Several considerations enter into my approach to such a project. The central of these is a desire to seek a nonimperialistic, nonpatriarchal Christian theology while at the same time understanding and maintaining the integrity of the Christian symbol system. I am led to this aim in several ways. One cannot be religious in the abstract. To be religious is to be religious somehow; religiosity is embodied in specific beliefs and activities. As chapter 2 will make clear, feminists are pointing to the importance of recognizing and valuing particularity and diversity. This book will examine what happens to the particulars of the Christian tradition in those pluralistic positions that seek more "generic" religious symbols.

Feminist theory has also pointed to the importance of understanding, analyzing, and proclaiming one's commitments. This book will explore the relationship among various commitments one might hold, and how such commitments might affect thinking about Christian theology. It will also examine some of the current questions concerning the particular and the universal, and to what extent and how one might continue to make claims for some universals. It is unfashionable these days to make claims for "truth." And yet, as I will argue, the Christian tradition—and other religious traditions—do make claims that are meant to extend beyond themselves and their own intra-

Christian perspective. Indeed, as I will also argue, to fail to acknowledge that religious traditions are making such claims beyond themselves is to trivialize them and to place their claims for ultimacy alongside much more mundane claims of taste, say, preferring ice cream to broccoli, or Bach to Beethoven.

Another reason for embarking on the current project is discomfort with each of the three proposed options of exclusivism, inclusivism, and pluralism as ways to understand Christianity within the world religions. Each seems to me to present problems of its own. Thus, I was seeking *at least* a fourth option. Schubert M. Ogden has recently argued that there is such a fourth option, and he sets out to show what that option might be.[8] This current book will not directly present cases for and against the three usual options and Odgen's proposed fourth option. Its central aims are different. Yet, as the argument of this book proceeds, the occasion to reflect on these various options will arise.

Can one identify oneself as Christian without being imperialistic about it? Is there a responsible Christian theological position that can lay claim to and claim truth for the central symbols of Christianity while at the same time maintaining the integrity and the possibility of the truth and salvific power of other religious traditions, and that can do so without so relativizing all those traditions as to say truth is only a function of context? And can one find such a position that also can claim to be nonpatriarchal? This book seeks to sketch a position in which the answer to all three questions is affirmative. Clearly, such a task is not easy. Nor do I wish to claim more for the results than one ought.

Both Christian theologies and feminist theories are diverse. No one position will be acceptable either to all feminists or to all Christians. Thus, although the task is large, the claims are modest. As a theologian, I present one way to look at Christianity within the plurality of religious traditions, a way that seeks to be both feminist and faithful to Christian tradition.

Many of the current discussions of religious pluralism that have arisen recently have been single-faceted; they have concentrated on one dimension of interreligious connection, often on the question of "truth." Or, as talking about truth becomes more and more an area of contention, focus shifts away from truth to moral action or justice. In this book I present a multi-faceted view of the possibilities for interreligious understanding. I argue that religious symbols, and here I concentrate on Christian symbols, make several sorts of claims at once, thus providing several points of entry into the tradition and several beginning points for mutual comprehension across boundaries of religious traditions.

I begin with feminist theory and criticism. Very few feminists have, as yet, entered into the debates on religious pluralism. Yet it seems to me that feminist thought offers several hints and resources for such debates. In chapter 2, I propose what some of those hints and resources might be.

One of the important lessons of chapter 2 is that one must begin with the particular and the specific. In terms of the Christian tradition, this means beginning with questions of christology. Christological questions have been seen as the most problematic in interreligious discussions between Christians and others. In chapter 3, I approach christology from the questions raised for it by feminism and the plurality of religious traditions. I look again at the foundational documents of the Christian tradition and propose a christology that seeks to be both responsible to the tradition and yet able to answer questions posed in our present context.

I argue that when we examine the earliest responses to Jesus, we see that the particular christological claims made for and about him can and should also be understood as specific embodiments of more general claims about God, humanity, the rest of the world, and what interactions among them would conduce to fullness of life. Here, my analysis discovers that claims about God's relationship to humanity also point to claims about God or ultimate reality in and of itself, and, further, raise the question of how reality as a whole is to be construed and valued. Following Clifford Geertz, this dimension is often called "worldview." Claims about humanity's response to God point to claims about what activities can and ought to be undertaken, thus raising questions about ethical activity or right relationship. But response to God is not only a matter of ethics, of action toward the creaturely. Humans have also embodied that response in such activities as ritual or liturgy, storytelling, music, and art. Again, following Geertz, this dimension is often called "ethos."

Beyond Christian Imperialism and Patriarchy

The question of fullness of life is not exhausted by mere descriptions of worldview or ethos, for the issues of value raised in both categories push us further. To ask what one can truthfully say about God, or ultimate reality within the context of reality as a whole; to ask how one should respond to God—these are important questions. The answers to them spell out in reasoned and reasonable form courses of thought and action. They eliminate certain barriers. But in the end, why do I respond? What grasps me? To what sort of value does my life contribute if I respond to a certain concept of God? In order for me to live human life to its fullest, is it sufficient to know that I am engaged in the right or just activity? How do we account for worship, for more than simply functional sacred spaces, for "religious" art or music? Ethics is not a sufficiently broad category in which to understand the value of the whole and the value and contributions of all its varied parts. Why has the category of "experience" become so central to feminist concerns? Here we enter into the realm of what has often been called aesthetics, into questions of what it means to experience something as worthy of enjoyment, as contributing to fullness of human life.

Although interreligious understanding might come to a quick halt if we compared the set of Christian symbols and doctrinal claims with other specific sets of symbols and doctrinal claims, and found them, on the face of it, incommensurable, discussion might well be able to be continued further at the level of these more general claims about God, humanity, the rest of the world, and the interactions among them that conduce to fullness of life.

Chapter 4 will deal with the question of God, beginning with concepts of God found in the Christian tradition. I will explore what claims about ultimate reality might be both appropriate to the Christian tradition and true. The issue of what it means to talk about truth in making religious claims is central here, in particular questions of what it might mean to make general or universal claims to truth and of how ideology affects claims to truth.

Chapter 5 will deal with the human activities implied by the Christian concept of God in terms of ethical activity directed toward others. It will explore whether and how human activities might be understood in terms of categories such as "justice" or the "good." It will examine how ethical acts have been tainted by patriarchy.

Chapter 6 will raise the broader question of aesthetics from a starting point within Christian tradition. Religious traditions, Christianity included, seek to persuade followers to certain kinds of ethical acts in the world. Beliefs and acts are also embodied, however, in forms such as ritual, prayer, story, music, and art. To be worthy of acceptance, Christianity or any other religious tradition needs to be experientially satisfying. It has to be able to grasp not only the minds but also the hearts of its followers. It needs to ask about the value or values of the whole to which individual parts of reality contribute. In what ways does fullness of life entail more than right belief and ethical action? Here I will begin with hints provided by phenomena associated with religious traditions whose central importance appears not to be exhausted by pointing adherents to right belief or right action—for example, ritual, prayer, music, art, and so on. In other words, I will look at hints provided by the contribution of aesthetic phenomena to religious life. The category of the aesthetic or beautiful will be defined broadly to refer to the creation of value and the satisfaction of experience or fullness of existence not only by and for humans but by and for others with whom human beings share the universe. Yet, as we will see, one cannot easily separate aesthetic phenomena from use in service of ideological ways of thought and life.

In chapter 7, the final chapter, I will come explicitly to the implications of the theological position sketched out here for the relationships of Christians to those of other religious groups. How do discussion of God and the category of "truth," human activity toward others and the category of the "good," and fullness of existence and the category of the "beautiful" expand the possibilities for a feminist Christian theology seeking to understand other religious traditions? I will also come back to the specific examples that are set out below. Throughout I will make use of the feminist critiques, hints, and resources raised in chapter 2.

Are There Universals?

The book begins with the specific, the particular, but much of its argumentation is more formal than material. Through formal argumentation I seek the more general or universal through the specific and particular. As the book proceeds, I will argue that one should not, indeed cannot, give up all appeal to the general or universal. However, I am not blind to the arguments coming from a variety of fronts that challenge the very possibility of the universal. Feminisms of various sorts challenge the false universals of patriarchy. Feminists have observed that the patriarchal way of seeing and constructing the world, placing most of the power and prestige in the hands of men (and a very few privileged men at that), is only one possible way of constructing relationships among human beings. Yet such has often been the pervasiveness of this way of constructing the world that patriarchal organizations of power have seemed and been treated as all-encompassing universals. The placing of power, including the right to interpret the world to others, in the hands of a few elite men, is not the only way in which the social and political relationships in the world can be construed. There are a multiplicity of other ways to see the world, and feminism is pointing us to those.

The category "men" has been a false universal, used to subsume women under generalizations that often do not apply. In terms of philosophy and theology, women often simply did not find themselves accounted for at all, except as part of "all men" or as adjuncts or afterthoughts. Thus, when philosophy spoke of "the experience of all men" or theology spoke of "the sin or salvation of all men," women began to see that they were not really part of the subject group. Either they were simply assumed to be part of the group, but no one thought to consult them to see if the statements about all "men" really applied, or they were ignored as unimportant to the enterprise.

As women in this generation came to recognize that their experience was not included in accounts of "men's experience," they also came to see the diversity of experiences had by women. False universals led many feminists to see the importance of particularity, the importance of looking at specific scenarios and experiences rather than subsuming them too quickly under a supposed universal. Women want to take charge of the naming or telling of their own experiences.

Recognition of the persuasive, often coercive, power of false universals masquerading as true universals has led feminists to be rightly suspicious of anything or anyone who makes claims to universality. Are women (and nonelite men and children) really included here? Recognition of the particularity and specificity of each individual woman's experience does not necessarily lead to a denial of the possibility of all universals, but it certainly leads to a suspicion of universals too easily attained.

The "universal" has often come to women as disembodied, an intellectual abstraction that takes little account of their lives as persons of flesh and blood. Disembodied and abstract universals, with their all-encompassing claims, have often led to a hierarchical dualism that values theory above life as lived, mind above body, thought above practice, men as representative of the mind above women as representative of the body. Such "universals" have seemed to many women to have no relation- ship to their actual lives, providing no account of their lives and offering no clues for living. Women have often experienced the negative impact on their lives of theories that purport to be neutral and generally applicable. They have been told that they ought to feel and think in certain ways because, after all, all "normal people" (read, men) feel or think thus-and-so. Thus, if women feel or think differently they are human misfits.

Historical consciousness has also made us more suspicious of universal claims. Once we began to recognize that history is made by humans and can be changed by humans, that there is no controlling power of God or fate or whatever, that social and political systems were human constructions and could be humanly altered, our lives were changed forever. Not only were humans responsible for historical events either directly through their specific actions, or indirectly through the past actions of others, these events could not be predicted in any specific detail with any certainty. The range of possible human choices in any given moment multiplied by the number of people and moments throughout human history gives infinite scope for possible outcomes. No universal can capture such variance and multiplicity.

In addition, not only is history made, it is seen, interpreted, and retold in any number of ways. And what is seen as important to recount, how it is recounted, for whom it is recounted, why it is recounted, and so on, also have infinite variations.

Not only the recounting of history in language, but the very fact of linguisticality also present a challenge to universality. Some would argue that all apprehension, all experiencing, is so bound up with particular linguistically embodied interpretations of that experiencing that the two are not separable. Experience is that which we interpret linguistically, which is experience-as-something-that-must-be-stated. The statement of my experience, my interpretation of my experience, is mine alone, and might or might not bear any resemblance to anyone else's interpretation of a similar (how could one ever say the same?) experience.

The possibility, indeed the actuality, of a multiplicity of recountings of the world and one's role in it have led some thinkers to the conclusion that there is no one world, no one "reality" which each person seeks to interpret. There are only "realities" as interpreted.

12   Although interpretations, linguistic renderings, are many and varied, these interpretations are not usually given in private or idiosyncratic languages. The language used, however adapted to the interpretations of the user, is meant for communication, for conversation. The language used is also language inherited, language used by others in other conversational or communicative contexts. As such, language is not neutral but carries with it a certain baggage, a certain history of its usage. As argued by thinkers such as Michel Foucault, our language already carries embedded within itself relationships of power and knowledge that are at times invisible to us but that govern much of our discourse by giving us particular ways to talk and providing us with categories in which to think.[9]

In addition to the diversity of experiences and interpretations that arises through history and language to challenge the possibility of the universal, some feminist thinkers such as Luce Irigaray, for instance, also point to the *différence* inherent in women's and men's interpretations and language. For Irigaray the gender of the speaker makes an inherent, not just a socialized, difference. Thus, there is no "universal" that cuts across gendered lines. The category "universal" pays no attention to gender but is, rather, the outcome of those who have the power to name it.[10]

Particularity and Universality Are Not Mutually Exclusive

All the above challenges to the possibility of the universal or the generalized make important points that need careful consideration. Indeed, a variety of ways exist to construct the world, and clearly some of those ways have been to the advantage of some people and the disadvantage of others. When we can conceive of alternate constructions of power and privilege, the world looks entirely different. But is the variety of social constructions infinite? Are all social constructions equally valid ways of seeing the world? What is social construction construction of? As the book proceeds, I will argue that, important as it is to see the human construction of social power, political relationships, and so on, it does not serve feminist interests well to argue that any one social construction is as valid as another. Certainly arguments for certain kinds of social construction and not others can be made on the grounds of the interests and well-being of women, and many feminists have made such an argument. I will argue that such a position is necessary but not sufficient to sustain the claims that I as a feminist want to make for a world that is changed to provide better for the possibility of fullness of existence for women.

Feminists are rightly wary of universals, having been offered a bill of goods that included so many false claims to universality. Indeed, the feminist move to particularity is a crucial first move to ensure that what is claimed has some basis in the real lives of more than a select and privileged few. Whether or not the move to particularity, and thus multiplicity or diversity, is the ending point as well as the beginning point will be discussed as the book proceeds. The existence of false claimants to universality does not, in and of itself, mean that there are no valid claimants to universality.

Clearly universals, if such there be, are not sufficient to account for life as lived. Universal claims, claims about all reality or all humanity, for instance, can only inform decisions on a particular and specific course of action. They cannot, by themselves, comprehend all the possible outcomes or know the possible results of a particular decision or course of action or process of thought. The universal without the particular lacks embodiment, it lacks concrete application. The universal has sometimes been seen to be the whole rather than an abstraction from the whole. When universals are a supposed substitute for the particular, when they are used to the exclusion of the specific, they become disembodied, disconnected from life. When, later in the book, I argue that some abstraction is necessary for

13

us to understand and communicate with one another as well as to ground the claims that we make, I do not argue that such communication, such grounding, is a substitute for the multiplicity and variety of embodied human life as lived. To argue the need for some level of abstraction is not to argue that the abstract is triumphant over the embodied and particular. Nor is it to argue that the abstraction is superior to the embodiment. Part of the problem with the disembodied nature of abstraction is that this disembodiment has been seen as of greater importance than the everyday life of embodiment. There is every reason to assume that one cannot actually have the general without the particular, but this assumption does not necessarily imply the impossibility of the general or universal. That the general has been seen as more important than the specific in a hierarchy of values does not mean that it must be so seen.

We cannot replicate a past event exactly. Once over, it will never recur. But our inability to replicate the past exactly does not necessarily mean that the course of history is totally random. There are certain constraints on what can happen in human history and in the history of the world. One such constraint is what has happened in the past. The past, although it can be interpreted in many ways and although its importance can be variously touted and understood, is in certain ways simply given as part of the material out of which the present comes to be, and it cannot be un-given. For example, despite those who try to deny it and those who try to ignore it, the sheer fact of the Holocaust, the killing of six million Jews, has changed Western history, both in its interpretation and in what the past presents to be interpreted, forever. The lives of millions were cut short, the lives of others changed forever.

Another constraint on history is our own embodiment and the embodiment or materiality of all that is. There are things that we cannot do in, with, and to our bodies or the bodies of others with whom we share the earth without destroying those bodies, those embodied selves, completely and utterly. Sometimes, perhaps, I can transcend my body, through imagining that it or I can do what I cannot do because my body/myself will not permit it. The possibilities for life in the world may be infinite, but they are not without constraints.

Historical consciousness has meant that most of us no longer believe that God or fate or some external force is controlling the outcome of all that happens. That all is not determined does not necessarily mean that everything is up for grabs. There may be continuities in history, universals, generalizations that can be made without entailing the notion that all must therefore be determined.

Interpreting Our Lives and Commitments

When we do express ourselves and interpret our lives, we do so linguistically. But is our interpretation all there is to our experiencing? In chapter 4 I will suggest that experience is more than our rendering of it in language, that one can distinguish experience from interpretation, and that such a distinction (without a separation) makes sense.

15

Linguistic interpretation, like historical consciousness, sees that particularities determine our specific and individual lives as lived. But, as demonstrated by the writing and reading of this very book, conversation is possible. Communication presupposes something shared by means of which a bridge can be built to one another. Although it is possible that the shared element is something that arises within a particular community, the fact that humans have tried (and succeeded?) to communicate despite radically different social, linguistic, and cultural backgrounds suggests more than a shared communal context. It suggests to me that there is something beyond language that binds humanity together. This argument will be further developed throughout the book.

Unlike Irigaray, I think the gendered *différence* of interpretation is socialized rather than inherent. If such difference is inherent, no communication between men and women is possible.

I would maintain that formal argumentation, searching for the general or universal within and through the specific, is indispensable for dealing with the particularities or specifics of our lives. I do not appeal to the formal to avoid the particular but to illuminate it. Communication and mutual comprehension depend on the ability to extrapolate from the particular. All theory generalizes about the particular, not in such a way as to substitute for it but rather in the hopes of drawing and evoking connections, thus opening the way for fuller understanding.

To illustrate the usefulness of formal argumentation for reflection on specific situations and thus, I hope, to obviate possible criticisms that the book is unconnected to life as lived, I offer, from my own experience, some concrete and specific examples of why the questions in the book are pressing practical as well as theoretical questions in the context of my own life. I am certain that situations of similar sorts arise in the lives of others. I will return to these examples in chapter 7 with a view to showing how the formal argumentation of the book provides some of the necessary resources for dealing fully with the particular issues at hand.

• Several years ago I was involved in planning for a series of Jewish-Christian dialogues in the city where I live. The pattern of the group had been to pick an issue or series of issues and explore the variety of opinions or actions that might arise in each tradition. I suggested that women might be a possible topic for the discussions. But no one else, Christian or Jew, wanted this topic. Instead, we chose poverty. As I reflected on this, it seemed to me that there was a collective fear of having to look critically both at ourselves and at others. We knew beforehand that there would be serious disagreement, and the group chose not to risk that. Instead, we knew from past experience we could find much common ground in dealing with the topic of poverty, and that seemed safer.

• In the Canadian province where I live there are two publicly funded school systems, a Roman Catholic system and a public system. Until a few years ago, the school day in the public system began with "religious exercises" of a Protestant Christian flavor. Protestant ministers were invited into the schools to be religious educators. Members of other religious groups began to object to the privileging of Protestant Christianity in a system attended by their children and funded by their tax dollars. In the debates that ensued, many Protestant Christians felt compelled to argue that this was a "Christian" province and therefore, Christian prayers were appropriate, the school system should continue to teach "Christian" values, and Christian holidays such as Christmas and Easter should continue to be celebrated with religious art and song.

• I teach a course entitled "Women and Religion." I have often invited women from a variety of religious traditions to come to the class to talk about their own experience of being a woman and an adherent of Christianity, Judaism, Islam, and so on. The students, most of whom come from secular, loosely

Christian backgrounds, feel free to criticize the religious and political choices of the Christian women. They are slightly more reserved about their criticisms of the Jewish women. Even though they have serious reservations about the choices made by some of the more traditional Muslim women who have come to class, they rarely voice those to the women who come. As they meet these women they come face to face with questions of the grounds on which we make our choices and on which we criticize the choices of another.

• In the last several years, my own denomination, the United Church of Canada, has been attempting to formulate a theological understanding of its relationship to other religious traditions. Not surprisingly, this has caused a great deal of debate. On the one hand, the denomination includes those who wish to continue the traditional Christian view that Jesus is the only, sole and sufficient savior for the whole world. On the other it includes those who think that we need to draw what is useful from a variety of religious traditions and that no one religious tradition should hold a privileged place.

• When I traveled to the West Coast of Canada in the summer of 1993, the major issue in the news was a blockade of logging roads to keep old-growth forest from being clear-cut. This blockade was organized by a diverse coalition of people. On one day the front page of the paper carried the story of the arrests, side by side, of Starhawk and an Anglican priest.

• In the Art Institute of Chicago, I stand in front of Marc Chagall's painting *The Praying Jew,* pondering its religious import for me, a Christian and a woman. What should I take from this painting of relevance for my own religious life and for my understanding of Judaism?

We shall return to each of these recounted experiences at the end of the book to see how the argument of the book might contribute to understanding these situations and to formulating human responses to these situations and others like them.

2
Feminist Analysis and Religious Pluralism

Women in the world's religious traditions have recently become an important topic for scholarly work. Their status and roles vary greatly from tradition to tradition and, within traditions, from one branch to another, and from one historical or social context to another. The state of scholarship about women in religious traditions also varies enormously, depending on *who* is asking *which* questions and *why.*

The state of the questions may vary but, when one looks at a religious tradition with the question of gender specifically in mind, some common threads emerge. Women in world religious traditions have been affected by patriarchy in its many guises. The contexts and manifestations have been different, but patriarchy has been a pervasive influence in many of the world's religious traditions.

Feminist Critiques of World Religions

Critical reflection on the patriarchy of religious traditions explicitly arose first within Christianity and Judaism in the West as women from within those traditions began to reflect on their own experiences and began to integrate their critical reflections into their scholarly work. In Islam, Hinduism, and Buddhism critical scholarly feminist reflections first arose from those who studied the traditions as scholars and outsiders to the traditions. There may well have been early internal critiques of patriarchy in these traditions that have not made their way into the scholarly literature. There are feminist scholars from within Islam and Buddhism who are seeking usable feminist reconstructions of these traditions.[1] Most of the feminist reflection on Hinduism of which I am aware has been done by non-Hindus.

One common concern of feminist critiques of world religions is religious symbolism within particular traditions, including which symbols are central or ultimate, rather than peripheral or dispensable. Discussion of symbolism often includes exploring dualisms, which divide things into two opposing categories and rank them hierarchically. Another common concern is the question of leadership and power. Who holds what roles within the tradition and how are these roles valued? What sort of power is exercised by members and officials of the tradition and who holds this power?

Feminist examinations of religious traditions also include a tradition's basic texts and teachings. Are these texts and teachings inherently patriarchal? Even if they are in patriarchal form, might they permit nonpatriarchal interpretations? How far has critique of the tradition been done by those inside and by those outside the tradition? How does one enact in the present what is considered central to the tradition? Is there a history that can be claimed or reclaimed as usable for women or in the liberation of women from oppression? What access do women have to the goals, values, and goods of the tradition?

Although it might be a subset of many of the above themes for discussion, the question of how sexuality and in particular women's sexuality is viewed in the tradition has been a sufficiently important theme for many women in a variety of traditions that it deserves to be singled out for special attention.

The status and roles of women in various world religions are not consistent within the traditions themselves. Branches and variations sometimes mean that women are regarded very differently within the same tradition. Geographic location and the variations of culture within it have resulted in wide variations in the status and roles of women. Class, caste, and economic status influence religious roles available to women.

Feminist critique of Christianity is long-standing, as are the many feminist efforts at the reconstruction of Christian theology in light of feminist critique. For example, the maleness of most traditional God-language has elicited much discussion.

Some feminists have become post-Christians because they see the symbol of God as inherently male. To move beyond the maleness of God is, for such thinkers, to move beyond Christianity.[2] Other feminists have engaged in searches for lost or almost lost female language about God, arguing that the tradition can and does encompass female language for and images of God.[3] Still others have sought to create or retrieve new female images of God and other images that do not have an explicitly male connotation.[4]

Likewise, much reconstructive effort has been directed toward the meaning of the maleness of Jesus. The dualisms that raise mind or spirit over body, male over female, clergy over laity, and so forth, have been much explored, in particular, by Rosemary Radford Ruether.[5]

Most mainline Protestant churches ordain women, but more conservative Protestant churches and the Roman Catholic and Orthodox churches use a variety of arguments against the ordination of women, based on tradition and on particular interpretations of those whom Jesus chose to be leaders in the early Christian movement. There has been extensive feminist discussion about whether women ought to aspire to ordination at all. For some feminists the idea of ordination smacks of an elitism that women ought not to buy into uncritically. More and more Christian women are studying theology at the graduate level, and even within the Roman Catholic Church growing numbers of highly educated women are teaching in theological colleges and universities. Within local congregations, because most of the members of churches are women, women have assumed most leadership roles. But in churches where women are not permitted in the central roles of word and sacrament, the power to interpret and enact the central rituals of the tradition is lost, and with it the ability to see oneself and be seen as central to the tradition.

Much debate among feminists interpreting the Christian tradition regards what role the texts and historical traditions ought to play in a nonpatriarchal tradition. Many feminists have appealed in one way or another to a central liberating message of the texts. Others have argued that the biblical texts might contain some useful resource material, but they should not be seen as normative. There have been many examples of reclaiming a usable Christian past by discovering women from the tradition who have been forgotten and by reinterpreting familiar texts through new eyes and with new feminist questions.

Sexuality, especially women's sexuality, has been a difficult topic in Christian tradition. Dualisms of mind over body, the ascetic tradition, fear of sexuality on the part of thinkers such as Augustine whose interpetations became central, the notion of woman as temptress—all these became part of a trajectory in Christian theology that associated women with sexuality and demeaned both. Feminists are pointing to other strands in the Christian tradition to overcome these negative views. The goodness of creation as attested in the Bible is often the basis of these rethinkings. A refusal to buy into mind-body dualism and its notion of a disembodied soul or spirit has been key to much feminist rethinking of sexuality. Feminists have recognized that it is fear of the power of women's sexuality and the power to give birth, rather than teachings central to the Christian tradition, that may have been fueling negative notions of women's sexuality.[6]

Jewish feminists have also begun the process of rethinking Judaism from a feminist point of view. Judith Plaskow's book *Standing Again at Sinai* is a sustained reflection on many of the topics that affect women's participation in Judaism.[7] Many Jewish feminists have dealt with the question of God-language and the assumed normative maleness of those whom the deity addresses and uses. As Rita Gross in an early article noted, "Beginning to address God as 'She' in addition to 'He' is a powerful reflection and indication of the 'becoming of women' in the Jewish context. The ultimate symbol of our degradation, of our essential non-Jewishness—which finds expression in all forms of Jewish life—is our *inability* to say 'God-She' or to create female imagery of God."[8] The solutions to the question of language and imagery about God vary, from using gender-neutral language to using male and female language to using language derived from a variety of goddess traditions to supplement traditional language.[9]

The various branches of Judaism have dealt differently with the question of women's leadership. Only Orthodox Judaism now refuses women as rabbis. Many women are choosing to be rabbis in Reform, Conservative, and Reconstructionist Judaism. The experiential implications of solely male leadership are powerfully dealt with by Laura Geller, who notes that people's first experience of her as a rabbi is a shock to their view of themselves and their religion.[10] Feminists have also questioned why a minyan ought to consist only of men.[11] Many Jewish feminists have argued that the "separate but equal" approach to women—that women have different tasks to perform, different prayers to say, different religious responsibilities centered in the home rather than in public—has not brought equality, because men's tasks, prayers, and responsibilities have usually been valued more highly.

How far the tradition can be and has been reinterpreted varies greatly within Judaism, but feminists have begun to reexamine Jewish law with feminist questions in mind.[12] In Judith Plaskow's comprehensive feminist reinterpretation of Judaism, the notion of Torah is expanded to include "women's words, teachings, and actions hitherto unseen."[13] Women need to claim their full presence at every part of Jewish history and seek unremembered texts and traditions or new readings of familiar texts and traditions that assume women's participation. Midrash is a useful category for feminists because it extends reflection beyond the categories of the biblical texts and highlights the figures on the edge, bringing them into fuller and more focused view.

Jewish attitudes toward sexuality have in some ways been more affirming of humans as sexual beings than has traditional Christianity. Sexuality has been seen primarily in terms of the goodness of God's creation. Yet women's sexuality has been controlled by countless restraints. "To speak of sexuality is to speak of women occasionally as fellow people—themselves desirous but subject to social restraint—but mainly as objects, as Others, as dangers to male moderation, as hazards to the balance and regulation that mark sacred order."[14] Many Jewish feminists have sought to reclaim their own sexuality and to overcome the ambivalence toward women's sexuality in the tradition, and this means reconstructing the patterns of relationship between people so that a healthy sexuality can flourish.[15] Plaskow argues that we need to recognize and reclaim the connection of sexuality to spirituality, seeing sexuality as an aspect of our life energy that allows us to reach out to and relate to others, including God.[16]

Feminist reconstructions of Christianity and Judaism have gone further to date than feminist reconstructions of Islam.

Feminist criticisms of Islam have often been from non-Muslims who have been acutely conscious that they speak as outsiders.[17] Also, because feminism in its present form began mainly in North America, there are serious questions about the cross-cultural relevance of feminist critique. In Christianity and Judaism, much feminist reformulation of the tradition was made possible because of general acceptance of the texts as historical documents to which historical criticism was applicable. The notion that there could be scholarly historical critique of the Qur'an is not acceptable to most Muslims.

In part because of Muslim prohibitions on imaging God, the question of the maleness of God has not arisen as a central matter for discussion. Riffat Hassan argues that God is not "thought of as male by Muslims in general."[18] I do not know of anyone who has reflected on the implications of the use of the pronoun *he* for God in the Muslim tradition.

Approaches to women and views of women in the Qur'an and Hadith have, thus, been mostly in the realm of rereadings or reinterpretations to show there could be alternative ways to interpret texts that have traditionally seemed negative to women. For instance, there has been much reflection on the Qur'anic verse 4:34, which is often appealed to as a source of male superiority over women. Verse 4:34 reads, in part, that "men are *qawwamun* of the affairs of women because Allah has made the one superior to the other and because men spend of their wealth on women." The Arabic word *qawwamun* has been variously translated as "protectors" or "managers" or "maintainers" or "having preeminence" or "masters" or "in charge" of women.[19] Those inclined to read this passage with the interests of equality in mind usually interpret it to mean not that men as a group are superior to women as a group, but that there may be particular instances where a man has more knowledge of the matter at hand[20] or that the man needs to guarantee security to a woman, who is doing the reproductive labor of childbearing.[21] Qur'anic passages that seem to imply the superiority of men and inferiority of women are read in the light of passages that seem to affirm the essential equality of men and women. For example, "The Believers, men and women, are protectors of one another" (9:71-72).

On the whole, although there has been some exploration of women's rituals and women's role in the mystical tradition, women have not entered into prominent roles of religious leadership in Islam.[22] Although it has depended on geographic and cultural context, women's sexuality has often been regulated by interpretations of rules and customs concerning veiling, segregation, and divorce. Virginity in brides has been greatly prized. Women's sexuality has often been socially controlled to keep women from what are considered inappropriate social contacts with men.[23] Yet even though such social control has been justified by appeal to Islam, if one looks to Muslims around the world one can see that interpretations and customs about veiling and segregation of women from men vary widely from place to place. Many Muslim women interpret the traditional verses that are seen to require veiling to mean that women should be modest, but what modesty is seen or said to entail may not mean the veiling traditional in some parts of the world.[24] Indeed, some Muslim women see both the veil and segregation of the sexes as goods that mean that women do not have to deal with the unruly sexuality of men.

Much of the available feminist interpretation of Hinduism comes from non-Hindu scholars. To my knowledge, although there have been feminist reinterpretations of aspects of Hinduism, no comprehensive feminist reinterpretation of the vast and varied Hindu religious traditions has yet appeared. In terms of symbols for the ultimate, Hinduism offers both goddesses and gods in abundant forms. Yet, as feminists began to realize, there is no direct causal connection between female deities and the status of women. There have been feminist reinterpretations of the goddesses of Hinduism[25] and feminists are beginning to look critically at the textual and ritual traditions.[26]

Many of the rituals of Brahmanic Hinduism are complex and require long preparation and training to be properly performed. Women have not traditionally been given that training. Women are expected to define themselves in terms of their marital status, the three phases of their lives being maidenhood, marriage, and self-immolation or widowhood; whereas men's lives are defined in terms of their relationship to the religious tradition, as studenthood, householdership, forest dwelling, and renunciation. Some rituals belong exclusively to women, but these have been passed down through oral tradition and have not been much documented until recently.[27] Some modern female gurus have emerged.[28]

As in many religious traditions, the chastity of women has

been greatly prized and guarded with strict rules. In the Vedic texts menstruation and pregnancy are equated with impurity.[29] Sexuality is seen as an impediment to the religious life and women have often been equated with sexuality. Thus, there is scope for feminist reinterpretations of Hindu women's sexuality.[30]

As Rita Gross points out in *Buddhism after Patriarchy*, because Buddhism is nontheistic, "there is no gendered Absolute or Supreme Being valorizing the male sex among humans as does the deity of male monotheism."[31] Gross sees the maleness of the historic Buddhas as a historical accident and a sociological necessity of patriarchal times. Many forms of Buddhism have an impersonal concept of Buddhahood, which, when it is manifest historically, has taken male and female forms. In addition, there are male and female mythic and symbolic models to which persons can appeal.[32]

25

In her feminist reinterpretation of Buddhist history and tradition, Gross draws on what she takes to be an essentially liberating core of Buddhist tradition even though that tradition has often taken patriarchal form. Gross applies feminist critique to central Buddhist notions to show that Buddhism is not only compatible with feminism but that, properly understood, the central Buddhist teachings lend themselves to feminist use.

Although orders of Buddhist nuns had virtually died out, there is in recent years a growing movement of Buddhist nuns. In addition, lay practitioners like Gross also argue for a rethinking of the place of the layperson in Buddhist traditions. More and more women are taking places of religious leadership in Buddhism, as spiritual and religious leaders, as organizers, and as scholars and teachers.[33]

There have been and continue to be varying Buddhist attitudes to sexuality in general and to female sexuality in particular. Traditionally the female body was seen as a temptation and as repugnant. Yet spirituality as freedom within the world need not mean renouncing or devaluing sexuality, so much as it means putting it in proper perspective. Gross argues that within Vajrayana Buddhism, where sexuality is part of the spiritual quest, the equality of male and female, man and woman, can and ought to be reclaimed.[34]

Some feminists, despairing of ever reforming patriarchal religious traditions, have sought to create (or, some would argue, to rediscover) traditions such as Wicca that are explicitly feminist in intent. These new religious traditions are many and varied. Wicca, for instance, is a name claimed by those who would embrace a wide variety of symbol systems loosely held together by belief in the goddess or gods and goddesses together, a principle of doing no harm, and a close connection to the earth. Other feminist religious options vary widely from one group of religious practitioners to another. Rather than apologize for feminism, such religious options are created by and around feminist values and goals. Thus religious symbols are female, or female and male together. Such traditions are, for the most part, oral, and in any event not binding on current belief and practice. Leadership is the leadership of women, often shared leadership, or women and men together. Sexuality is embraced as a good, as part of the goodness of the world.[35]

What Feminism Can Offer

Although recognition of our religiously plural world is widespread, not many women have entered into the religious and theological discussions of religious pluralism.[36] As a woman and as a feminist, however, I ask in what ways a feminist contribution to these ongoing discussions could be illuminating, even crucial to fuller understanding.

When I use the terms *feminist* and *feminism* here, I use them broadly to indicate types of analysis, critique, and constructive formulation that take seriously the imbalances of power and privilege that have been meted out on the basis of gender. Feminists ask about the dominant position of men and the subordinate position of women in our society and others, about what its causes might be, about what factors serve to perpetuate it, and about what alternatives there might be to the status quo. Thus, I mean any position that recognizes the gender imbalance of power and privilege in favor of men and that seeks to redress that imbalance in some way. Clearly, feminist positions are diverse, and I do not want to ignore that diversity. But here I am asking a broad question, and thus a broad definition of feminism is in order.

Feminism can make four contributions to the ongoing discussions of religious pluralism. First, feminist concerns can act as a corrective to Christianity before anyone even enters into interreligious discussions. Second, many feminist concerns are shared *across* religious boundaries, thus giving common beginning points and common ground for thought and action. Third, since most women are not in positions of power and authority in their own religious traditions, if feminists encourage interreligious discussions among women, the conversations that take place will go beyond religious "officials" talking only of officially sanctioned theological positions. Fourth, the feminist emphasis on particularity seems to point to the richness and multivalence of religious symbols, discouraging the use of and search for "generic" religious symbols and terms. I will discuss each of these contributions.

The first two contributions run parallel to each other insofar as the ties that feminists can forge across religious lines are often borne of recognition of common oppression. Thus, attempts to reform within and the making of bonds without should be simultaneous processes. The commonalities of oppression arise in a variety of ways. For instance, within Christianity, and within many other religious traditions of the world, oppression is based on patriarchal perceptions of woman's bodiliness, especially centered around female sexuality.

It was not until I began teaching a course on women and religion that I noticed how prevalent some form of menstrual taboo is within religious traditions. Within Protestant Christianity, the associations of menstruation and religious taboo have been masked, but still within Roman Catholicism there lingers the notion, much more pronounced in the Christian past, that a menstruating woman will pollute the altar, and this is certainly one of the reasons for the prohibition against altar girls. Judaism, Hinduism, and Islam all have their historical menstrual taboos, too, connecting menstruation with pollution and warning men against association with menstruating women lest they too be polluted.

Women are often seen as a sexual distraction to men, an oft-cited reason why women cannot assume roles of religious leadership. In Christian tradition, we have the image of Eve (or at least the dominant interpretation of her) to remind us of our role as temptress. Not so long ago a male theological student said to one of his female colleagues that he could not concentrate on her sermon because her beauty was a distraction for him. Within many religious groups (some Christian, Jewish, and Muslim groups), women are separated from men in worship, so the women will not distract the men. Jewish feminists have often remarked that any male Jew who can with discipline keep the 613 commandments ought to be able to concentrate on worship, whether women are present or not. To my knowledge, there has been no comparable reflection on the men distracting the women! In religious traditions, women's sexuality has often been fenced in by strict boundaries and rules, including rules about conduct and dress. For example, in 1 Peter:

> Do not adorn yourselves outwardly by braiding your hair, and by wearing gold ornaments or fine clothing; rather, let your adornment be the inner self with the lasting beauty of a gentle and quiet spirit which is very precious in God's sight. It was in this way long ago that the holy women who hoped in God used to adorn themselves by accepting the authority of their husbands. (1 Pet. 3:3-5)

In virtually all the world's major religious traditions the leadership and the power accrue to men. Where there are female leaders, they are in the minority. The roles that have been considered appropriate for women have been carefully circumscribed and defined. Women have begun to explore the commonalities attendant to this lack of religious roles or carefully circumscribed roles, whether by actual religious legislation or by tradition.

Feminists within a variety of religious traditions have begun to raise questions about the central religious symbols and imagery of their traditions. Although the imagery varies among religious traditions, it is often male, or if there is male and female imagery and symbols, they are often perceived and valued differently according to gender. Feminists have begun to ask both about the effect on women of the varied weighting of such symbols and also what the social and political implications of such symbols have been.

Recognition of these commonalities leads to two further observations. First, the commonalities provide one good reason to be suspicious of imperialistic claims for one's own religion, in the case described here, Christianity. I cannot without much thought and questioning simply accept Christian claims to religious superiority. Second, the commonalities also lead us to view with more skepticism claims that thoughts and practices that place women in subordinate relation to men are intrinsic to a particular religious tradition. Is this subordination divinely "revealed" or is it simply an effect of patriarchy given religious blessing?

The bonds forged by acknowledging some of the commonalities of women's experience across religious lines are further cemented by seeing the possibilities for common activity. Indeed, it may be the fact that women from a variety of religious backgrounds find themselves engaged in common action that leads toward the discovery of other commonalities. One way to talk about what feminists are seeking (not indeed just for women) is "justice," seen, for example, by Marjorie Suchocki as centering on "inclusiveness of well-being," where well-being has to do with "concrete reality manifested in concrete communities."[37] Cross-cultural and interreligious work for justice includes such activities as working for food and shelter for the poorest of the poor (mostly women and children), working to eliminate violence against those who are already disempowered by society, working for peace in war-torn areas in which soldiers are not the only victims of war, and so on. For example, one of the concerns that unites the women of Asia across religious lines is a concern to combat prostitution. In Asia many young girls are forced into prostitution because their families cannot afford to care for them, and often families choose to care first for sons. Prostitution in Asia is fueled by rich tourists who pay high prices for sex, but the sex trade is controlled by men while the women themselves make very little. Concern for prostitution goes far beyond a concern for sexual morality, and analysis of prostitution goes far beyond the notion that women "choose" to be prostitutes.

Women's work for common causes likewise goes beyond intrahuman concerns to concerns for the world as a whole. In many cultures women have been aligned or identified with nature. Probably because of their role in giving birth, women have often been seen as more "earthy" or more closely connected to nature than men. When nature and culture are distinguished, women are usually associated with nature and men with culture. Although women are rightly wary of being totally identified with nature, the traditional connection might well forge ties to foster wholeness not just for women themselves, but for all that is.

Concerning the third contribution of feminism to discussions of religious pluralism, when women are involved in preparing for or taking part in interreligious dialogue it increases the likelihood that the discussions will take place not just on the level of officials talking to officials about official stances. Thus a more varied and variegated picture of any given religious tradition might well be presented. Women, by their very presence in interreligious discussions, often question the "official" stances of their traditions. We also, by our presence, force a rethinking and redefinition of who really counts in religious community. Whose actions and whose words are taken to be central to and normative for a given tradition? What counts as "authority" and who is allowed to define it? We broaden the range of what might be considered important to say. In Hinduism, for example, some specific rituals are performed only by women. These need to be studied on the same basis as those of men. Such a contribution of women helps us to see that religious traditions are not monolithic but diverse. In Chris-tianity this might well result in more emphasis on what laypeople do and say and less on what clerics do and say.

Feminism and Christianity's Particularity

Within feminism, there has always been an emphasis on the particularity of experience, a recognition that because women's experience has been ignored in so many areas, something vital has been lacking. Feminism has encouraged us to focus on the concrete, the particular, the diverse. Feminist theorists have rightly pointed out that too often supposed "universals" left a lot of people out of account.[38]

This feminist appeal to concreteness and particularity leads, I would argue, to a "hermeneutic of suspicion" concerning one of the common moves many Christian theologians have made in their attempts to overcome the imperialism of traditional Christian theologies.[39] I am speaking of a solution that encourages Christians to move away from christocentrism (employing a religious symbol system centered in Jesus as the Christ) to theocentrism (centering on God) or to soteriocentrism (centering on salvation).

The move away from christocentrism takes a variety of forms. Its appeal is that it is seen as a way to avoid an imperialistic view of Jesus, a view that recognizes him as the only, sole, and sufficient savior of the whole world and because of that subordinates all other religious traditions to Christianity.

Many theologians warn against the dangers of christocentrism. Paul Knitter, for instance, worries that the term *christocentrism* implies that Jesus is normative for all religious experience.[40] Thus, he first favored "theocentric christology" (a view of Jesus that is centered on God) and then "soteriocentric christology" (a view of Jesus centered on the concept of salvation) because Knitter thinks we should follow the example of Jesus, who was theocentric (Knitter's first term for Jesus' stance) or soteriocentric (a word Knitter has used more recently) in his own religious practice. John Hick argues that we need to move from seeing the religious universe as centered in Christ and his gospel to a "Reality-centered conception with its pluralistic implications."[41]

Although I have my own feminist suspicions about making a move away from at least some form of christocentrism too quickly, some feminists have embraced this move. Rosemary Radford Ruether, for instance, sees the claim that Jesus is the Christ to be inherently anti-Jewish.[42] She sees Jesus essentially as a Jewish prophet who, like other Jews of his times, looked for a messiah to come. "Jesus should not be said to fulfill all the Jewish hopes for the coming Messiah, which indeed he did not. Rather, he must be seen as one who announced this messianic hope and who gave signs of its presence, but who also died in that hope, crucified on the cross of unredeemed human history."[43]

Ruether's concern about anti-Judaism is a legitimate one. Many christologies have treated Judaism as the incomplete and subordinate sister. Christians have perpetrated horrendous acts upon Jews in the name of Christianity.

But should Christianity move away from at least some sort of christocentrism? Can it do so and still remain Christianity? Even Paul Knitter recognizes that "the pervasive message of the New Testament is undeniably christocentric."[44] I believe that in their laudable desire to avoid anti-Judaism Ruether and the others have too easily passed over the particularity and specificity of Christianity. Historically speaking, Christianity is not a Jewish sect, as it would be if Ruether's view of Jesus were the view that came to be centrally held and shared. Nor is it the religion *of* Jesus. Rather, it is the religion *centered on* Jesus. Knitter, Hick, Ruether, and others see that Jesus is historically important for the beginnings of Christianity, but they have virtually ceased speaking of him as the Christ and of seeing Christianity as centered on claims about Jesus. I would argue that they have also ceased to take seriously the experiences of early Christians.

One can ask what it means to claim that Jesus is the Christ, and one can ask whether this claim is true. One can decide that Christian claims about Jesus are inherently imperialistic. But, I believe, one cannot understand the particularity of Christianity without accurately affirming its distinctiveness. What distinguishes Christians from those of other religious traditions, particularly from Jews, is the claim that Jesus is Christ or Savior or some other such maximal claim (as distinct, for example, from the claims that Jesus was a good man and a prophet). This argument will be pursued in greater detail in the next chapter.

To say that Christianity must be christocentric, however, does not mean that there is only one way to be so. Nor does it mean that Christianity is the only path to salvation or the only way to be authentically religious. What I am cautioning against is what I take to be a questionable move away from historical particularity on the basis of a laudable aim.

Feminist stress on the concrete and particular is important, even crucial, for understanding the current religiously plural world. Every religious tradition has its particular history and its particular set of religious symbols and images. "Religious symbols are those phenomena, events, roles, and persons in everyday life which put us in mind of our transcendent ends or our ways of realizing these."[45] Traditions, I would argue, can be defined on the basis of having a central symbol surrounded by a cluster of primary symbols.[46] Primary symbols may vary some in importance from time to time or place to place, but it is the central symbol that gives the tradition its identity and provides for continuity through historical change. These very particular and concrete symbols give rise to a richness of interpretation that may be complex and varied. They are not univocal. And, in many ways, this is what gives them the lasting power to evoke from human beings a religious response.

It is entirely possible that some religious symbols or entire religious symbol systems cannot be rescued from patriarchy or from imperialism. The point is that one only knows this if one grapples with the particular and the specific.

Now, in pointing to the importance and power of diverse

religious symbol systems, I do not want to argue that they cannot be compared or that all religious traditions simply have to be accepted as equal and true. Fear of imperialism has led some theologians to a relativist position in which all religious traditions as seen a priori are equally true or valid because reality is irreducibly multiple or because truth is only truth relative to a given context. Theologians like Raimon Panikkar and Tom Driver take such a position.[47] In the name of recapturing so much lost diversity, feminist theologians might be tempted to this same course of action.[48]

Yet feminists, although we are rightly wary of false universals, need to think through carefully what is lost if we claim that there are no universals at all. If feminism is to effect the reforms it seeks, feminists must be prepared to argue that feminist analysis is more than one way among multiple equally valid ways of seeing the world. Marjorie Suchocki says:

> I reject, however, the possibility of entering into dialogue with no judgments whatsoever.... What is called for is not a nonjudgmental dialogue with other religions in light of the relativism of belief systems, but a shift of judgment from ideological ground to ethical ground, along with an open recognition of the conditioned nature of the norm of justice we bring, and a commitment to critical exploration of the norm in the very dialogue wherein it is brought to bear.[49]

In chapter 4, I also argue that we cannot give up the possibility of making claims to truth as well as to justice. If the universe, if reality, is one, then we must endeavor to understand and to speak the truth of it, albeit in historically conditioned speech.

The question of particularity and universality is a crucial one both for feminists and for anyone interested in questions of religious pluralism. Feminists recognize that patriarchal societies have failed to take seriously the experience of half the population. Those concerned with Christian imperialism realize that Christians have often failed to countenance as genuine any religious experience outside the Christian symbol system. How do we value the diversity of women's experience, how do we value the diversity of human religious experience, without simply reducing experience to one group's experience that cannot be understood by outsiders or individual experiences that are the experiencing subject's own and that therefore cannot be understood by anyone else?

Although the "discovery" of the vast diversity of women's experiences has led feminists to be much more wary of making claims for "women in general" than we used to be, the argument that one cannot understand someone else's experiences will not in the end sustain feminism. If women's experience is irreducibly and incomparably plural, then nothing binds women together against patriarchy. We are divided by our experience, not united by it. Also, if no one but myself can understand what I have experienced, then how can men be blamed if they do not understand what I am trying to tell them about my experience of patriarchy?

As a feminist I write and talk not just to hear myself, but because I think that those who read or listen to what I say can understand what I am trying to tell them and might even change accordingly. We feminists are just wasting our breath if, in the end, no one can ever understand what we are trying to say from our own experience.

There are parallels here to the issues involved in interreligious understanding. A diversity of symbol systems does not necessarily lead to an inability to enter into discussion and comparison. We need to ask what a given religious symbol system is communicating, and then we need to see how that compares to what other symbol systems are saying. It is at this point that there arises a need for a more generic language. Here is where ideas such as "theocentrism" or "soteriocentrism" might be usefully employed.

Generic symbols such as Hick's "Eternal One" or "Reality" are crucial to the enterprise of interreligious understanding, crucial to a philosophical reflection on the meaning and truth of religious traditions. But while they are a tool, they are not, I think, religious ends in themselves. The religious symbols cannot be given up for more generic symbols without evacuating a good deal of their richness and evocative power. One can understand and seek philosophical commonalities without needing always to talk in philosophical terms.

We cannot pass over diversity too quickly. If we do, either in talking of women's experience or in talking of religious experience, we run the risk of losing something crucial, and we clearly run the risk of losing touch with the concrete, the specific, and the particular. We have to keep coming back to the particular, always measuring what we say by it, always being wary of universals that come too easily.

But the particular by itself does not allow us the possibility of communication, of interconnection, or recognition of commonality. It is the very recognition of commonality that allowed for the rise of the women's movement. When an individual woman was paid less than a man, when she was passed over for promotion, when she was not completely and totally fulfilled by keeping house, when she was battered for no reason, she thought she was an individual case, an aberration. When women started to recognize their collective experience of being paid less, passed over, undervalued for their work in the home, and abused, a movement was born.

Likewise, recognition of common humanity and common human questions, however diversely asked, has led to a dissatisfaction with Christian imperialism.

To posit, intuit, recognize commonality is one thing, and to articulate it is another and more difficult and demanding task. Both in feminist thinking and in thinking about religious pluralism the challenge is to hold the particular and the universal in tension, not to let the commonalities get swallowed up by myriad diversities, not to jump too soon to pseudo universals. The way to the universal is through the particular and not around it. Feminist thought has helped me to discover this and apply it to my thoughts about religions.

3
Understanding Jesus within Christianity

Feminism urges us to begin with the particular. When one is dealing with religion, this urging makes good sense. To be religious is not to be religious in general, but religious in some particular way. Religious people symbolize their religious impulses in particular and specific ways; they adhere to particular beliefs and courses of action; they celebrate specific rituals.

In the Christian tradition, to begin with the particular is to begin with christology, that is, with our understanding of Jesus, to whom Christians have given the title *Christ* or *Messiah*. In Christian understanding of other religious traditions and in interreligious discussion, the major issues have arisen around how Jesus the Christ is understood and portrayed to others. "I am the way, and the truth and the life. No one comes to the Father except through me" (John 14:6). This assertion is placed on Jesus' lips in the Gospel of John. It has been interpreted to mean that unless one makes an explicit commitment to Jesus Christ, one cannot receive salvation. It has often been taken to be the central and last word on Christian attitudes to those of other religious traditions.

Christology has also presented serious problems for feminists. The maleness of Jesus has been used, for example, as central to the argument against the ordination of women in the Roman Catholic Church. If the male Jesus is the only or the fullest revelation of God, what does this say about femaleness?

In this chapter, keeping in mind questions raised by feminism and by the current religiously plural situation, we look again at Jesus Christ and outline a christology that is both responsible to the Christian tradition and yet responsive to contemporary questions occasioned by pluralism.

Theologies That Eschew Christocentrism

Some theologians have suggested that instead of formulating a Christian theology with Jesus the Christ at its center (a christocentric approach) we must begin to fashion theologies with God at the center (theocentric) or with salvation as central (soteriocentric), or theologies where activity aimed at bringing about liberation is central. John Hick, Rosemary Radford Ruether, and Paul Knitter all propose that if other religious traditions are to be taken seriously Jesus must no longer stand at the center of Christian theology. Christians must be willing to give up their specific claims about Jesus in favor of more general claims about God, about salvation, or about ethical activity.

John Hick accomplishes his goal by suggesting that Christians need to concentrate less on the specifics of the tradition that separates them from others and more on the more generic "Ultimate Reality" or "the Eternal One" pointed to by Jesus, who is one savior among many. For Hick there is no place in interreligious dialogue for what he calls "purely confessional dialogue." In purely confessional dialogue, "the Christian speaks from within his own conviction that God has entered decisively into human history in the person of Jesus Christ."[1] In comparison with this entry, all other revelation is secondary.

Hick proposes to concentrate on the universal because the particular can only be divisive. Various religious traditions are thus differing responses to "the Eternal One."[2] In our pluralistic situation today, Christian response to "the Eternal One" still takes place through Jesus, "our living contact with the transcendent God"; but we must give up as poetic imagery all talk of incarnation.[3] "We can revere Christ as the one through whom we have found salvation, without having to deny other points of reported saving contact between God and man. We can commend the way of Christian faith without having to discommend other ways of faith."[4]

Although he does think that one can evaluate religious traditions in a variety of ways,[5] Hick does assume rather than argue that "the different world religions have each served as God's means of revelation to a different stream of human life."[6]

Ruether also assumes that "true revelation and true relationship to the divine is to be found in all religions. God/ess is the ground of all beings, and not just of human beings."[7] Ruether wants to broaden the ways in which revelation, even within Christian tradition, is seen. As a Christian she worries that to call Jesus "the Christ" is inevitably to be anti-Semitic and inevitably to rate other religious traditions as negative in comparison to Christianity. As a feminist, she is concerned about Christian revelation coming in the male form of Jesus.

Ruether does not speak of Jesus as "the Christ." She sees Jesus as "a first-century rabbi...who became a prophet and critic of established religious authorities. Betrayed by powers of religions and state, he was executed by Roman officials as an insurrectionist."[8] Not only in the context of interreligious discussion, but also in the context of Christianity, Jesus is not the last word on revelation for Ruether. She thinks that he points beyond himself. Christianity should not concentrate on Jesus but on "Christ":

> Christ, as redemptive person and Word of God, is not to be encapsulated "once-for-all" in the historical Jesus. The Christian community continues Christ's identity. As vine and branches Christic personhood continues in our sisters and brothers. In the language of early Christian prophetism, we can encounter Christ *in the form of our sister.* Christ, the liberated humanity, is not confined to a static perfection of one person two thousand years ago. Rather, redemptive humanity goes ahead of us, calling us to yet uncompleted dimensions of human liberation.[9]

The goal of Christianity is liberating activity, in particular, liberating activity on behalf of women.

Paul Knitter proposes that we should not be christocentric as the New Testament is, but theocentric as Jesus himself was.[10] In *No Other Name?,* he presents what he calls a "nonnormative christology" that understands Jesus "not as exclusive or even as normative but as *theocentric,* as a universally relevant manifestation (sacrament, incarnation) of divine revelation and salvation."[11] In his essay "Interreligious Dialogue: What? Why? How?" Knitter opts for the idea of soteriocentrism to replace theocentrism:

In this model, the center or the "Absolute," if we can still so speak, is not the church or Christ or even God but salvation or human liberation—the welfare of humanity and of this earth, the promotion of life and the removal of that which promotes death.... In more expressly Christian terms, the framework for a Christian theology of religions is not church, Christ, or God but *soteria* or the kingdom of God. Of course church, Christ, God are not simply discarded or kept on the sidelines of dialogue; rather, they are "aufgehoben": transformed and understood anew in their relation to the kingdom.[12]

Here he concentrates more on Jesus as prophet. "If fidelity to our traditional confessions is primarily a matter of following Jesus the prophet-servant of the kingdom, we will be, at least theoretically, open to the possibility of other prophets. What matters most is that the kingdom be promoted, not that Jesus maintain primacy."[13]

As I will argue below, I have much sympathy for the view of Jesus as universally relevant manifestation of divine revelation, as articulated by Knitter. What is not clear to me is why it is so important to deny the christocentrism of Christianity and to see Jesus simply as a prophet. Indeed, as Knitter himself argues in *No Other Name?*, the New Testament is christocentric.

Hick, Ruether, and Knitter worry that to focus on Jesus as the Christ is thereby to take an exclusivist position and thus without critical reflection to rank Christianity above all other ways of being religious. All three think the focus of Christianity ought to be elsewhere. For Hick, it ought to move beyond narrow confessionalism to a focus on Ultimate Reality. For Ruether, the focus ought to be on the activity enjoined by Jesus the prophet, in particular, activity liberating to women. For Knitter, the focus is on God or, later, on salvation.

Even if one does move to theocentrism or soteriocentrism there is no guarantee that other traditions will be taken seriously. Indeed, if one does not take seriously the integrity and specificity of Christian religious symbols but wishes immediately to make them over into something more generic (as do Hick and, to a somewhat lesser extent, Knitter), what guarantee is there that other religious traditions with their own specificities will be taken seriously? J. A. Dinoia, aptly I think, names such positions as those of Hick, Knitter, and Ruether "christological minimalism." He notes that such pluralistic stances imply that it takes an "ensemble" of religious traditions to describe religious life, that no one religious tradition is sufficient, or that one must appeal to a set of categories above and beyond any and all religious traditions.[14] Religious traditions give specific and perhaps distinctive content to such concepts as Ultimate Reality or salvation. If one begins with specific ways to describe this Ultimate Reality or salvation or whatever the central concepts of a given tradition are, one runs less risk of creating an abstraction with no discernible content. To begin with some assumed common claim or common experience may well be to begin with a false universal. If one begins with the particular and works outward, the danger of false universals seems to be somewhat lessened.

In many ways Ruether does take the particularity of the Christian tradition seriously. Her view of Jesus, although different from the one that I will present, is based on her reading of the specifics of Christian origins. What she has in common with Hick and Knitter, however, is the view that if Christianity centers on Jesus—indeed, for Ruether, if Christianity claims Jesus to be the Christ—it will automatically take the form of exclusivity, thereby being unable to affirm the full value of other religious traditions.

The position for which I argue in this book takes seriously Hick's, Ruether's, and Knitter's concerns, and it shows how their insistence on Ultimate Reality, liberation, and salvation are crucial to understanding christology. But it will take issue with the notion that exclusivism is only overcome if claims about Jesus as the Christ are displaced from the center of Christian concern.

Theologies That See All Truth as Relative

Some theologians who face the bewildering variety of ways of being religious take another tack. They allow that Christians can be committed to Christianity as true but that the truth of Christianity, like the truth of any other religious tradition, is relative: Christianity is true for me. A commitment to Christianity means that one looks at the world in a particular way. But others see the world in other ways.

Raimon Panikkar provides a notable example of this approach. For Panikkar religious traditions are sui generis. They have their own ways of speaking and their own boundaries and cannot be easily compared. "There is no absolute center. Reality itself is concentric inasmuch as each being (each tradition) is the center of the universe—of its own universe to begin with."[15] Panikkar argues that the truth is neither one nor many. Truth is plural because reality is plural. Something is only true or false within its own parameters. There is no one reality to which all religious traditions refer.[16]

Likewise, for Alan Race, one can make a commitment to Jesus Christ in our present age of recognizing multiple religious traditions as long as one also recognizes that claims about Jesus are intra-Christian claims and therefore not applicable to non-Christians:

> Jesus' "decisiveness" is viewed as primarily related to those who have received the light of God made known through Jesus, and developed in one particular cultural form. Jesus is "decisive," not because he is the focus for all the light everywhere revealed in the world, but for the vision he has brought in one cultural setting.[17]

I will explore more fully below and in chapter 4 the question of what it means to claim truth for statements about religious belief. Here it is sufficient to note that in such understandings as are held by Panikkar and Race, the claim "Jesus is the Christ" really means "Jesus is the Christ *for me.*" If Jesus can be said to be the Christ, that claim can only be said to be true for a certain group of people, at a certain time in a certain cultural setting.

Limitations of Moving beyond Christocentrism

The plurality of religious traditions vis-à-vis the traditionally exclusive claims of Christianity does present important issues for which the writers quoted above have sought solutions. These issues concern how Christians, making their commitment to Christianity, can understand themselves and others while not imposing that commitment on the rest of humanity. They allow that many others are sincerely committed to other religious traditions and do not evidence the desire or need to convert to Christianity. They grant that the claims traditionally made by Christians have not taken seriously either those of other traditions or of women in general.

The first solution examined above proposes that Jesus and claims about him are not really the heart or center of Christianity. The second solution names Jesus as the center of Christianity, savior for Christians; but it holds that the claims Christians make do not have any validity nor ought they to have any validity for those who are not Christians.

Christoph Schwöbel, in assessing Christian stances toward other religious traditions, makes the important point that both exclusivism and pluralism fail to do justice to the interplay of particularity and universality in the Christian tradition. Exclusivism emphasizes particularity without taking the universality of God seriously. Pluralism emphasizes universality without taking particularity into account:

> The pluralist approach, contrary to its avowed intentions, seems to tend to develop a picture of the universal and ultimate noumenal focus of all religions transcending the particular concrete religions or of a common anthropological constant underlying all particular religious expressions, which allows their distinctive particularity only a penultimate and preliminary status.[18]

Thus, not only is Christianity's particularity compromised, so is the particularity of all other religious traditions.

Many feminists have argued that it is precisely because of the particularities of Christianity that feminists need to abandon it entirely. Daphne Hampson, for instance, claims that Christianity is neither true nor moral. Hampson does not think it is credible to claim God's revelation in a particular person rather than more generally given to all. Further, christology can never bring fullness of humanity for women. "Christology gives a male human being a status which is given to no woman."[19] When the maleness of Jesus is highlighted as crucial to understanding his role in Christianity, feminists understandably worry that in this case particularity is being used to argue for the greater value of maleness over femaleness. Such worries are exacerbated when the particular tradition is also seen to include or imply a male God, a male priesthood, and in general a set of dualisms that value mind and spirit over body, men over women, humans over nature. Yet feminists are also rightly wary of false universals, "universals" abstracted from the particularities of, at best, only one-half of the human race.

Yet changing the center or locus of Christianity to something or someone besides Jesus does not do justice to Christianity as an historical movement. Christians, when they make claims about Jesus may well be making other sorts of claims as well, about God, salvation, and liberation, for instance. But historically these claims and the Christian movement grew up around Jesus, and many of the central claims made by Christians have been claims about Jesus.

What I propose to do, therefore, is to look again at the earliest traditions about Jesus. We are pushed back to these traditions by particular questions, in this case questions raised by feminism and by the plurality of religious traditions. We look at the early traditions and to the christologies implied by them to see what ways there might be to handle the issues raised. We begin with the particulars of the Christian tradition.

The Jesus of the Biblical Texts

The only access we have to Jesus is through texts; and, with the exception of a very few historical references, these texts are told and recorded by people interested in the stories because they have responded to Jesus. Christology, the branch of Christian theology that has concerned itself with reflection on Christian claims about Jesus, can take a variety of forms, as it has over the course of Christian history. I choose to go back to the earliest texts, the biblical texts, and to the earliest strands of those texts as they have been discerned by recent criticism.

Searching for the earliest strands of tradition about Jesus does not mean that one can get back to a "historical Jesus." One cannot discern with certainty what Jesus said, did, or thought. All the records we have about Jesus, even the very earliest ones, are already responses to Jesus.[20] Thus, they are already christologies, even if of an implicit sort (rather than the more explicit and developed christologies of later texts such as John's gospel or the even later text of the Council of Chalcedon). All reflections on Jesus are important for believers today. I go back to these earliest strands, however, because these strands are foundational for and constitutive of Christianity. The earliest responses to Jesus constitute the material upon which later christological reflections are dependent.

The Jesus to whom we have access in the biblical texts is a Jesus in relationship or interaction with others. Some scholars, while recognizing this fact about the biblical texts, argue that one can get back beyond this response to a "historical Jesus."[21] Despite all the sophisticated methodology for trying to come to an empirical-historical Jesus, one still has no real access to him that is not already witness of faith. This is not, however, a problem for Christian theological reflection. Christianity is not the religion of the historical Jesus, but the religious tradition that grew up around and because of Jesus. To understand the faith to which the earliest respondents to Jesus felt themselves called is to come to an understanding of the faith to which subsequent followers are also called.

The Earliest Layers of Biblical Tradition

Many scholars are engaged in attempts to get back as close to Jesus as the biblical texts will allow. Even if one argues as I do that one cannot get back to the "historical Jesus," the earliest layers of the textual tradition are constitutive for what follows. Here I am dependent on the recent work of biblical scholars, in particular that of Marinus de Jonge and John Dominic Crossan. Curiously enough, de Jonge writes virtually an entire book on the earliest responses to Jesus, then in the final chapter asks in what respects this earliest response reflects Jesus' own views.[22] He leaves to theologians questions about what to make of all this today.[23]

De Jonge sees the earliest responses to Jesus discernible in Q (the traditions of Jesus' sayings employed by Matthew and Luke, and common to them) and in the sources of Mark's gospel as implicit christologies. In Q:

> Jesus is portrayed as a unique envoy of God who has inaugurated a new era in God's relation with Israel and the world. His appeal, his promise, and his claim on people, as well as their response to him, continue to be of crucial importance.[24]

In the pre-Markan tradition, "Jesus was the man who spoke and acted with direct authority. His words remain authoritative, and his message is to be proclaimed by his followers who may heal and exorcise in his name."[25] In the earliest sources, "the emphasis is on radical obedience to the summons issued by

Jesus, and on complete trust in what is offered and promised by God through him."[26]

John Dominic Crossan finds in the earliest strands of tradition a Jesus who proclaimed a brokerless kingdom, not a future apocalyptic kingdom, but "a present ethical...realm,"[27] a sapiential, peasant kingdom. "What was described by his parables and aphorisms as a here and now Kingdom of the nobodies and the destitute, of mustard, darnel, and leaven, is precisely a Kingdom performed rather than just proclaimed."[28] The kingdom to which Jesus called his followers, proclaimed in a variety of verbal forms, and performed in eating and healing, was a "radically egalitarian one."[29] It did not include only or even primarily the socially desirable but included "nobodies and undesirables"[30] and thus called all the principles of the social order and privilege of the time into question:

> He was neither broker nor mediator but, somewhat paradoxically, the announcer that neither should exist between humanity and divinity or between humanity and itself. Miracle and parable, healing and eating were calculated to force individuals into unmediated physical and spiritual contact with God and unmediated physical and spiritual contact with one another. He announced, in other words, the brokerless kingdom of God.[31]

Crossan discusses the importance of the "performance" of Jesus, and by that he means that Jesus drew others into relationship with him.[32] He makes God and the realm of God alive and present. Among the earliest texts Crossan discerns are texts that express the present nature of the reign of God (for example, "The kingdom of God is already among you"); texts that enjoin immediate response (for example, "You have ears, use them!" "Love your enemies and pray for those who abuse you"); texts calling people to new relationship with one another (for example, "Whoever does not hate his father and mother cannot become a disciple to me"); and parables eliciting immediate action (for example, the parable of the wedding banquet).[33]

Although Crossan takes the social consequences further than does de Jonge, both see Jesus primarily as one who calls others to respond to God through him. The call to respond to God is a call to act, to live one's life in a particular way so that trust in God is enacted in the world. Jesus is experienced as one who makes a claim on the lives of others. The importance of these earliest strands for the questions raised by feminism and religious pluralism will be explored below.

Early Views of Jesus as Implicit Christologies

Present christology cannot be read directly from the earliest traditions about Jesus, yet these earliest traditions are constitutive for christology today. It is possible, of course, to build christologies on later developments in the history of Christian theology. For instance, christologies often have begun with the declarations of the Councils of Nicea or of Chalcedon, reading the biblical texts expecting to find and therefore finding the fully human, fully divine Jesus, the second person of the Trinity. As important as these conciliar definitions have been to illuminating who Jesus is and might be for us, we need to go behind them as far as possible to their own sources in the scriptural witness. These definitions are themselves responses to earlier interpretations of Jesus and speak to issues and concerns for their own times. The concern to get to the earliest traditions is not a concern to get to Jesus "uninterpreted" but to understand the effect of Jesus on his earliest followers, the response he evoked in them. For it is only *through* their experience of him that we experience him today. Our access to Jesus is only through the witness of faith, not alongside it.

In the earliest traditions, Crossan and de Jonge do not find explicit christologies with specific titles applied to Jesus, yet very early Jesus came to be interpreted with such titles. Some have argued that because Jesus would never have applied such titles to himself, the Christian tradition should not do so either. Christianity should be the religion *of* Jesus, such interpreters would argue. But we do not have direct access to the religion *of* Jesus. We have access to Jesus at all because, even from the earliest traditions, interpretations of him show him in a central role with regard to the reign of God he proclaimed, that is, they contain christologies, even if implicit ones.

A crucial thing to notice about these earliest traditions is that, because the christologies are not explicitly articulated in terms of titles or theological claims about Jesus, our attention is not first drawn to *Jesus*, it is first drawn to his effect on those who listened to him and *experienced* the inbreaking of the reign of God through him. In other words, Jesus' first followers did not become interested in him abstractly, as one of unique metaphysical makeup. They became interested in him because of his effect on *them*.

Crossan and de Jonge agree that central to the proclamation and action of the Jesus of the earliest tradition is the kingdom and the summons to respond to it through Jesus. Both Crossan and de Jonge tend to concentrate on Jesus as the one who issues a summons and evokes response. But the one who does the summoning, as they sometimes notice and sometimes do not, is not Jesus but God. The kingdom Jesus enacts is not his own kingdom but God's. The people who respond are responding to the grace of God they experience through Jesus, not to some charismatic personality. The followers of Jesus did not just hear *about* the kingdom, but through Jesus they experienced it in their lives. The summons to the reign of God is the summons of God to faith, not faith as belief in certain doctrines or concepts but faith as trust, *fiducia*. God's grace, God's love, is experienced by Jesus' followers; and when they tell the stories of their experience, they open that same experience to those who follow.

Such faith or trust also implies an interrogation, a demand. To respond in faith is not merely to assent in the abstract, but to commit oneself to enact the reign of God one has experienced. Another way to speak of the call and response experienced through Jesus is to speak of it as a call to salvation. Karl Rahner sees salvation as a two-way process. The first side is God's gracious move toward us, the totally unmerited offer of God's grace and love. The second side is the chance human beings have to respond to that grace, to enact it in their lives as faith working through love. "The divine history of salvation, therefore, always appears in the human history of salvation; revelation always appears in faith." [34]

When we look at the earliest texts about Jesus (or other texts about Jesus, for that matter), we can see that they are not just descriptions of who Jesus is, they are witnesses to the effect of God's grace experienced through him. Encounter with Jesus has changed the lives of those who tell and retell stories about him, not just provisionally but ultimately. And they understand this encounter and its effect as having their source in God. In Jesus, those who encounter him discover the ultimate source, means, and ends of their lives. They come to an ultimate rather than a provisional answer to the question: from whom and through whom shall we live in order to bring about fullness of life?

The grace of God enacted in Jesus is a grace for all. Women are explicitly included both in terms of the examples used in the earliest texts and in terms of the audience addressed. The message of the gospel is not first of all a message about Jesus, it is a summons to participate in the reign of God. If the brokerless kingdom is as Crossan suggests, then Jesus, male human being that he is, is not its broker for women or for anyone else. Jesus was not experienced by those who encountered him as the restriction of God's love but as its fullness. The earliest texts do not suggest any particular emphasis on Jesus' maleness or on maleness as normative for humanity.

To understand the Christian witness to Jesus in the way that has been suggested here is to see, as Schubert Ogden argues, that the point of christology is an existential one, that is, it answers not just the empirical question, "Who was Jesus?" but the religious question or question of faith, which has to do with "the ultimate meaning of one's very existence as a human being."[35] The central concern of christology is the ultimate meaning of my life in relation to God. As Ogden, following Clifford Geertz, sees it, this religious question has two aspects, named by Geertz "worldview" and "ethos," and by Ogden "metaphysical" and "moral." The metaphysical aspect of the religious question asks about "the meaning of ultimate reality for us"; the moral aspect asks about "the authentic understanding of our existence authorized by ultimate reality."[36] Thus, according to Ogden, religious traditions make their strictly metaphysical and strictly moral claims first as existential claims, as claims about the meaning of God in my life and how I ought to live in response to God in faith working through love.

To mention the metaphysical or strictly universal claims one can make about God does not address fully the existential relationship with God through Jesus Christ that Ogden sees as the point of christology. Human life in the world in response to ultimate reality or God is more than just human responsibility to one another or even to other creatures.

Response to Jesus on the part of his earliest followers often took the form of activity toward or for the neighbor. But it took other forms as well—as praise offered to God, telling again the story of what Jesus had done, or forming community. Fairly quickly these immediate responses became formalized in particular titles and ritualized in particular liturgical behaviors, in prayers, songs, art. The summons of God through Jesus was not just a way to think, nor just a way to act toward others. It was a life-changing experience that grasped and inspired all aspects of one's life. It was a change of outlook or attitude. It was, in the terms of Friedrich Schleiermacher, not just knowing or doing but "feeling,"[37] or perhaps better in today's terminology, experiencing. The whole area of "feeling" or experience often remains unanalyzed in christology.

Response to religious experience takes not just the form of direct action toward the human or nonhuman other, but also of worship, story, music, or art. Such expressions might well be analyzed in terms of their intellectual coherence or credibility, and in terms of the activity toward the other they inspire. But such analysis does not fully account for the human experience of creating or participating in such forms. Questions of the "true" and the "good" must be viewed in relation to a question about the general satisfaction of life, about what it means to experience something well or satisfyingly, a question that might be seen as one of "aesthetics."[38] Exploring the aesthetic dimension of christology will further address the feminist concern that Christianity must speak to women's experiences and must do so in a holistic fashion. In chapter 6, I explore in more detail the relationship between aesthetics and questions of truth and ethical goodness, especially in relation to feminist critiques and concerns.

Jesus and Salvation

What is the relationship between Jesus, whom Christians claim to be the Christ, and salvation? For those who adopt an exclusivist position, one can only come to salvation by an explicit encounter with Jesus Christ and by an explicit acceptance of the salvation he offers. Thus conversion to Christianity is necessary for salvation.

For the inclusivist, salvation comes about because of Jesus Christ; the grace God offers for salvation is the grace of Jesus Christ. Yet the grace of Jesus Christ might also be offered to others via other means or vehicles of revelation. Thus, although one may never explicitly encounter Jesus Christ, every offer of

God's revelation that comes to one is already the grace of Jesus Christ because it was in Jesus Christ and in him alone that God became incarnate, thereby extending the fullness of God's salvation for the first and only time. All other offers of grace or salvation are based on God's grace and final revelation of Godself in Jesus Christ.

Karl Rahner's view of grace and salvation is such an inclusivist view. The incarnation in Jesus Christ is the "final cause" of God's grace. All grace is Christian grace. Thus Jesus Christ is savior of all who accept God's grace, whether they know it explicitly or not. Hence Rahner's provocative phrase, "anonymous Christian." In the view of Rahner and other inclusivists, Jesus Christ is "constitutive" of salvation.[39] All salvation is wrought by Jesus Christ; all humanity is saved through the agency of Jesus Christ. This gives Christianity, as the religious tradition that explicitly receives and recounts the central and constitutive revelation of God, a certain priority over other religious traditions. One may not need to be explicitly a Christian in order to be saved; one may appropriate God's grace through some other religious tradition, or through no particular tradition at all. But Christians are those who explicitly recognize the source or cause of that salvation, whereas others only experience it implicitly, at second hand, so to speak. Thus, only Christians have the fullest possible congruence between the faith they explicitly espouse and articulate and the lives they lead. According to an inclusivist position, although other religious traditions may reflect and articulate the grace of Jesus Christ in their own categorical terms, insofar as grace is only properly understood as the grace of Jesus Christ, no other religious tradition can be true in the sense of correctly articulating an explicit understanding of religious experience.

What is the salvation offered through Jesus? Through Jesus, God summons hearers to respond to the imminent reign of God, to respond to the demand that God places before them in the neighbor, and to enact that grace, the reign of God, in their lives. The salvation offered through Jesus is composed of two elements: the divine call and the human response to that call. What Jesus presents to those who listen is God's love, God's grace, the reassurance of human longings to be valued, loved, cared for. The message of Jesus, proclaimed and enacted, is that God offers this love freely to all. This offer of love before we do anything to deserve it is also a call to respond, a demand to us to enact the love we have experienced. Christians have experienced this love, this grace, this call in Jesus whom they call the Christ.

A number of points challenge one to reflect, however, on whether Jesus, the one in whom God is experienced by his first followers, is the only possible way in which such experience of God's grace and love is available to humanity. The enacted or performed message of Jesus focuses on the free and freely given character of that grace, on the fact that it is for all, not just for some. If Crossan is correct that the message of Jesus is to proclaim and enact the brokerless kingdom of God, then to speak of Jesus as its sole arbiter limits a grace he proclaimed as limitless. The grace, the reign, is God's grace or reign, and it is God's unbounded love that is experienced in and through Jesus. Jesus calls his hearers to respond to God.

Jesus can be experienced and proclaimed as savior, as bringer of salvation, even as incarnation of God (see further discussion of this below) without necessarily affirming him as the one by whom salvation is constituted. The biblical tradition before Jesus recounts a particular experience of God's revelation, grace, and love. It recounts the necessity of human response in ritual, obedience, and prayer. The texts about Jesus do not indicate that what Jesus taught was to be seen as brand-new and never before known. Yet responses of Jesus' followers show that they felt themselves addressed anew and that the good news in the gospel call to repent, believe, enact grasped them in ways that they had not before experienced. In the earliest stories about Jesus, and even in many of the later stories, people are called not to belief in certain doctrines or concepts but to faith, to trust, to a new way of life.

If the question answered by christology is primarily one about the ultimate meaning of my existence as a human being, it is conceivable that there are other answers to the same question that bring about the same salvation Jesus brings and enacts. (It is also conceivable that there are quite different answers to that question, as we shall see.) Although Christians experience salvation when they encounter Jesus, the grace they encounter need not be restricted to Jesus as its only source or conduit.

Biblical texts are often cited to show not only that Jesus brings salvation but that there is no salvation until and unless

51

Jesus brings it. The two Gospel texts most often cited are Matthew 28:18-20 and John 14:6. The passage from Matthew about all authority having been given to Jesus and commissioning his followers to make disciples of all nations is considered a late passage, an addition by the evangelist in light of the community to which he is writing and its situation. After the destruction of Jerusalem, and after Jesus is rejected by Jewish leaders, Matthew needs to emphasize the worldwide character of Jesus' mission.[40] John's gospel is already a late composition, and it too reflects a break between Judaism and believers in Jesus. The passage about no one coming to the Father except through Jesus is a late assertion that can also be interpreted according to its context. Both texts, therefore, indicate not the first responses to Jesus but later reflections on these responses. If one takes the earliest stratum of the synoptics as normative (as I do), then the lateness of these texts makes a difference to how one should view them.[41] And both allow for broader interpretations than are often given them when they are quoted out of context to support the opinion that all must hear and respond explicitly to Jesus in order to be saved.

The passage in Matthew must be read side by side with yet another Matthean passage, Matthew 25:31-46, which places the emphasis not on what one says, but on what one *does*. In this story, God's judgment is meted out not on the basis of confessing Jesus, but on one's feeding the hungry or clothing the naked. The passage in John's Gospel needs to be seen in light of John 1, which emphasizes the Word, present before and active in all creation and ultimately incarnate in Jesus. John 14:6 need not be read as, "No one comes to God except by knowing and confessing Jesus"; it could be read to say that one comes to God only through the agency of God's Word, present to the whole world from its beginnings.

Communities that have experienced Jesus as savior, especially those concerned to set themselves over against others who have rejected Jesus, begin to associate him with any possibility of salvation. They begin to talk of their savior using the best and highest terms they know. They have received good news through Jesus, and they want others to have the same experience. Krister Stendahl describes this as "love language."[42] It makes maximal claims for the one who has been savior to them. It is akin to saying of a loved one, "You are the most beautiful (or the kindest or the best) partner in the world." Yet in the Gospels salvation is still God's free and gracious gift, which requires the one who accepts God's grace first to respond in faith and life rather than to make a particular confession about Jesus. This point is made in a text that Crossan finds to be a very early one:

> A woman in the crowd raised her voice and said to him, "Blessed is the womb that bore you, and the breasts that you sucked!" But he said, "Blessed rather are those who hear the word of God and keep it!"[43]

The concept of God's love or grace is constrained and diminished if one restricts God's grace or at least its only full expression to a particular historical time and place. To say God gave only partial revelation but not full revelation at other times or places is to conceive of a God who freely withholds Godself from all of creation until a certain point in time. If revelation is the revelation of Godself, the revelation of God's grace and love for us, it is difficult to know what it would mean to speak of partial and full revelations in any event, at least from God's side. An all-loving or all-gracious God can hardly reveal Godself as only partially loving. And how could one give content to the notion that God partially (rather than fully) reveals that God is all-loving or all-gracious?

To hold that humanity, both before and after the historical incarnation, were saved by virtue of the incarnation in Jesus Christ is to hold a view of history wherein an event in one century can affect events that happened before it. Thus, through God's plan for all of history, something that happens in the first century of the Common Era has a salvific effect that extends backward to the beginning of human life. As will be explicated further in the next chapter, a different view of history entails the co-creativity of both God and creatures in a process wherein the outcome of the free choices of creatures cannot be known in advance, even by God, and therefore no particular historical event could have a salvific effect on something prior to itself because no particular historical event could be assured to happen. Speaking of the incarnation as having an effect on events before it is different from espousing a point of view that sees the trinitarian God at work from creation and throughout the world, the grace of God freely offered to God's creatures as the grace not simply of Jesus but of the second person of the Trinity, the Word, Sophia.

Schubert Ogden makes a useful distinction between Jesus as constitutive of salvation and Jesus as representative of salvation. Whereas Rahner claims that the event of Jesus Christ causes or constitutes the possibility of all salvation, Ogden argues that

> for any appropriate understanding of the Christ event, it is so far from being the cause of salvation as to be its consequence. The only cause of salvation...is the primordial and everlasting love of God, which is the sole primal source and the sole final end of anything that is so much as possible.[44]

Ogden claims that Jesus Christ decisively re-presents God's grace, that is, he makes the meaning of God for us "fully explicit."[45] The possibility of salvation is not constituted by Jesus but by God's all-encompassing love, which is always and everywhere available to us. What Jesus does, however, is to present again that love in an explicit or focused way to those who might have lost sight of it or begun to question it:

> Jesus, they [the earliest witnesses to him] claimed, is the one through whom both they themselves and then, by means of their witness, all of their own hearers as well are decisively re-presented with the gift and demand of God's love, and hence with the possibility of authentic existence in faith and returning love.[46]

Jesus can be said to decisively re-present God because in and through him we can come to know the truth about God and about God's relationship to the world. (This sort of claim for Jesus can and must be evaluated on the basis of the more general reflections about God that will be undertaken in the next chapter.)

If Jesus re-presents rather than constitutes God's offer of grace or salvation to humanity, it puts the question of the maleness of Jesus into interesting perspective. If God's grace is re-presented in Jesus, presumably it could be re-presented in other ways and forms. If Jesus does not constitute revelation, then neither can Jesus' maleness be seen as in any way central to or constitutive of revelation. Nor can the maleness of Jesus be in any way seen as identifying God more with maleness than with femaleness, as Jesus' Jewishness does not identify God more with Jews than with Gentiles. When Jesus is said to re-present God, then, although one must examine how to speak of this God who is re-presented, one can in no way assume that the gender of the re-presentative is crucial to the re-presentative function.

The existential nature of the question christology answers means that the crucial focus is not on Jesus but on the relationship between believer and God that Jesus evokes. In the Christian tradition, Jesus is crucial to that relationship, for it is Jesus who calls it forth by re-presenting God's grace. But the relationship is also brokerless (to use Crossan's word) insofar as through his enactment of God's reign, people were brought into direct relationship with God. If Jesus re-presents God but does not stand between human beings and God, then he should no longer be seen as male mediator of God to women.

55

The Humanity and Divinity of Jesus Christ

If Jesus is to be seen as decisively re-presenting God's revelation rather than constituting that revelation, what does this imply about traditional ways of speaking of Jesus Christ in the Christian churches? In particular, what does it imply about speaking of the humanity and divinity of Jesus Christ? Because claims about the humanity and divinity of Jesus Christ or about the incarnation of God in Jesus Christ have often been taken *necessarily* to imply claims about Jesus as the only, sole, and sufficient savior, theologians who do not hold an exclusivist position are likely to see Jesus as a good human being, perhaps even the best possible human being. In this way they either shy away from any language implying divinity or they seek to describe Jesus' divinity as equivalent to being the "best possible human being in intimate relationship with God."

Leonard Swidler, Stanley Samartha, and John Cobb seek christologies that recognize the importance of Jesus for Christian faith, do not make him constitutive of all salvation, yet allow that claims made for him are true (not just simply true for those who believe in him already). For all three, Jesus Christ is the center of Christian life:

> Christians need to be quite clear about the basis of their faith, their identity in Christ, and the specificity of their Christian contribution. The distinctiveness of Christian mission becomes alive to Christians, and its motivation transparently clear to neighbors of other faiths, when the ethical and social concerns of the church in the world are recognized as stemming from God's saving activity in Jesus Christ.[47]

Understanding Jesus within Christianity

For all three, it is Jesus' own faith, his own closeness to God, that justifies the claims of divinity made for him. Leonard Swidler, for example, speaks of the divinity of Jesus in terms of the fullness of what it means to be human:[48]

> Jesus was so completely open to all dimensions of reality, to all being—as all human beings are in principle—that he was totally suffused with an inpouring of being in a "radical" way which included the "Root" of all being, God. Thus he was thoroughly human because he was divine—through and through—which is evidenced in what he thought, taught and wrought.[49]

For Samartha, to speak of the divinity of Jesus means that Jesus becomes the *darshana* of God and leads us to a new *dharma*, and Jesus can do this because of his own faith.[50] Samartha talks of a "bullock cart theology," wherein Jesus accompanies us through life rather that parachuting in from above.[51] John Cobb sees the Word of God present throughout the world. That presence is "uniquely realized in Jesus," in Jesus' closeness to God.[52] Thus, for all three thinkers Jesus can be called the Christ and can be seen as divine because of his own relationship to God.

The desire to present a credible view of the divinity of Jesus Christ is an important one. Swidler, Samartha, and Cobb recognize that it does not do justice to what Christians have traditionally claimed for Jesus to ignore claims about his divinity. Yet their claims for the divinity of Jesus all revolve around the faith of Jesus or his intimate union with God. But the earliest texts about Jesus do not give us access to his faith or to the inpouring of God into his being. The texts are witnesses of faith in response to Jesus that recount his effect on those whom he encountered; they are not witnesses to Jesus' own faith.

Thus, it can be suggested that the divinity of Jesus does not lie in claims about his own personal life, but in claims about his effect on others. When people responded to Jesus, they responded to God. When people encountered Jesus, they experienced the claim of God upon them. Jesus was *sacrament* of God, the direct experience of God re-presented to them, not someone acting on God's behalf. To refer to the divinity of Jesus is to reference experiencing the boundless love of God through him. This means that the divinity of Jesus is not some substance joined on to his humanity. Rather, one experiences Jesus' divinity through and because of his humanity. That one experiences God in and through Jesus' humanity need not necessarily mean that this is the *only* way to experience God.

If Jesus re-presents rather than constitutes salvation, if in his divinity he decisively re-presents but does not exhaust God's salvific grace, then speaking of Jesus' divinity need not be problematic for feminists. Speaking of the divinity of Jesus as I am doing here does not divinize maleness. The grace of God which encounters me in Jesus is not restricted in its appearance or functioning to Jesus. In the same way, to speak of the divinity of Jesus is not to restrict the notion of divinity to Jesus nor is it to say that because he is the sacrament of encounter with God he is necessarily the only such sacrament.

57

Also, as Carolyn Walker Bynum points out, there is no simple relationship between the gender of a religious symbol and the messages about gender internalized from that symbol. Nor do gendered religious symbols simply reflect cultural assumptions about gender. One must always ask "for whom" does a symbol mean and how does it hold meaning?[53] For instance, the presence of goddesses in Hinduism does not have a direct causal effect on the social structure of India, giving women parity with men. And vice versa, the social structure of India does not totally control the interactions between gods and goddesses. The impact of the gender of a symbol is more complex than a direct correlation between symbol and social structure.[54]

In the case of Jesus, then, one cannot look only at his maleness, one must also look at the context in which the meaning of Jesus is interpreted and how that meaning is interpreted. Bynum's point suggests that no symbol is simply and inherently patriarchal. Clearly, Jesus as male symbol has at times in the history of the church been used to serve patriarchal ends. But if we understand the earliest texts correctly, if we notice that the biblical texts speak of Jesus as human, not as male, if we remember that in the patristic period stress was placed on the humanity of Jesus, not his maleness (what is not assumed is not healed), then there opens an alternative (and earlier and constitutive) history when Jesus' maleness is not emphasized or really even noted as important. Thus, that Jesus was a male human being may or may not be counted as important in interpreting his significance. Indeed, that his maleness has been emphasized at many points in Christian history, in particular, in positions against the ordination of women, is ample reason for feminists to look seriously at the impact of Jesus' maleness. What I am arguing, however, is that Jesus cannot be rejected as savior figure on the basis of his maleness alone without asking if that maleness must necessarily function to bolster patriarchy in church and society.

Further, within the tradition Jesus is associated with Sophia, the Wisdom of God, who is portrayed as female in the Hebrew Bible.[55] While Jesus can be said to incarnate the grace of God, to be the grace of God to those who encounter him, he can also be said to incarnate the Wisdom of God, Sophia. Male human being though Jesus was, the female symbol of Sophia can also be associated with him.

Why Be Religious at All?

Why not abandon religious symbols entirely and simply live one's life on the basis of the more general claims they imply? As important as it is to state the general claims implied by religious symbols and to understand how such symbols can be communicating something credible to us, the symbols evoke a response at the level of the whole person, cognitively and affectively, that the abstract rendering of their meaning does not always accomplish. In the case of Christianity, the symbol of Jesus Christ invites and creates a relationship between the believer and the divine that is merely spoken *about* in theological language. Mircea Eliade, for example, argues that images and symbols say more and bring people together more effectively and genuinely than analytic language.[56] Paul Ricoeur claims that religious language cannot be simply or correctly reduced to literal speech:

> My deepest conviction is that poetic language alone restores to us that participation-in or belonging-to an order of things which precedes our capacity to oppose ourselves to things taken as objects as opposed to a subject. Hence the function of poetic discourse is to bring about this emergence of a depth-structure of belonging-to amid the ruins of descriptive discourse.[57]

Whether poetic language in religion is as irreducible as Ricoeur implies is a matter for further discussion. But the point is sound: one of the functions of religious symbols is to engage us, to draw us into the purview of the ultimate reality being presented by them.

We are not religious in general, we are religious in particular and concrete ways, as we have seen. Although religious symbols make claims about and connect us to the universal, they accomplish this through particular symbols and communities of women and men before us who have shared and found meaning and truth in those symbols. Through the symbols and the historical communities that have shared them our identity and commitments are partially formed.

Conclusions

Christians use specific symbols to express their religious experience and beliefs. In particular, as I have argued, they focus on Jesus as the Christ. Christians make claims about Jesus as the Christ and the effect that he has on them. They portray these claims as true not just for themselves but in general. Yet in an age where Christians cannot simply ignore the religious lives of others who do not share their symbols, how can they proceed? When we recognize that Christian claims about Jesus as the Christ are existential claims, claims about the ultimate meaning of our existence as human beings, we realize that it is then necessary to see Christianity not just as a unique set of religious symbols incommensurate with any other. Christian claims can be further analyzed in terms of the meaning of God or ultimate reality for us and our response to God. The latter analysis includes the ways in which the relationship between God and humanity conduces not just to moral action but also to the fullest satisfaction or enjoyment of life. That Christian claims do point beyond themselves to more general claims also opens the way to a Christian stance for understanding other religious traditions and expressions.

Putting Christian religious symbols alongside those of another tradition may seem to be comparing two quite disparate entities. But much more scope for discussion appears when those symbols are seen as claims that can be further analyzed in terms of our response to ultimate reality. Thus, one can claim and affirm the particularity of the symbols and can continue to use those symbols in all their particularity without necessarily claiming that those symbols are the only way in which the answer to the existential question could be expressed. One does not need to give up or water down one's own religious symbols to respect those of other traditions and to allow others to value theirs. Recognizing that the symbols point beyond themselves to other claims means that one can enter into dialogue or discussion with another tradition at several junctures rather than just at the point of the symbols. It also challenges the assumption that religious symbols *per se* exclude rather than the way in which those symbols are used.

This proposal does not mean, however, that every set of religious symbols makes the same claims or that every set of religious symbols is as adequate or true as any other. Such claims would require further analysis. In keeping with the aims of this book to work from the particular, I propose to look at various aspects of the existential question to which christology is an answer and, thereby, to see what grounds for dialogue with other traditions we might discover.

The Christian answer to the question, "From whom shall we live in order to bring about fullness of life?" is, "God." Thus, the next chapter will turn to the question of what Christian belief in God entails and how the God of the Christian tradition might be understood in terms of new feminist and pluralist questions. I shall explore the question of God in itself, with a view to considering what can credibly or truthfully be said about God in view of current discussions about truth claims. I shall also note that experience of God, and of reality as a whole, points toward an aesthetic aspect or dimension of the existential question.

Chapter 5 explores human response to God in terms of its moral implications within the Christian tradition. Activity in response to the Christian witness might challenge patriarchy and be a beginning place for interreligious understanding.

Chapter 6 examines response to God that might be construed as more in the realm of aesthetics than of morality. I will show that christology has aesthetic implications insofar as it points to an enjoyment or satisfaction of experience more all-encompassing than the categories of truth and goodness alone would seem to suggest. I will draw together the strands pointing toward aesthetics into a coherent whole that places the beautiful in relation to questions of truth and goodness and shows how discerning an aesthetic dimension in Christian symbols is important to the continued credibility of these symbols in light of questions arising from feminism and religious pluralism.

I am not looking as, Raimon Panikkar does, for functional equivalents of symbols across religious traditions. Rather, I seek to see how one might compare and contrast the more general claims made by Christians when they affirm Jesus to be the Christ with claims made through the symbols of other religious traditions, thereby providing a more nuanced view of Christian self-understanding that may serve well the project of understanding and relating to others.

4

The Christian God
and Truth

Claims about Jesus, we have seen, answer the human question about the meaning of our existence and what conduces to fullness of life. In answering this question, christological claims invoke God as the ultimate source of that meaning and that fullness.

The God of whom we hear in the earliest stratum of the Christian tradition is a God of grace and love who summons people to faith.[1] The grace or love of this God is boundless; it encompasses all humanity, even all creation. No one is outside its purview; nothing is outside the love of God.

This is a God of relationship, to whom it matters what happens to creation. God is described as a personal God, one who loves, cares, and enters into relationship with each and every one of God's creatures. All human beings, indeed all creatures, are the object of God's concern. This God knows and cares about the fate of both the sparrow and the human.

God desires the best, the fullest existence for all God's creatures. This desire is focused in the concept of God's reign wherein unexpectedly new relationships will be brought about. This is a God in whom love and judgment are joined. Love is universal, but those who will not repent are judged accordingly. Those who are last will be first. All laborers in the vineyard will receive the same wages, regardless of the time they joined the workforce. One is responsible to one's neighbor, and *neighbor* is an all-encompassing term.

This God is often referred to in male images. But there are occasional female images for God in the early strata, for example, a woman who rejoices over a found coin and a woman making bread. It is also worthy of note that the incidence of the use of the term *father* for God, which has so influenced the overall Christian image of God, comes predominantly from John's Gospel and not from the early strata of Christian witness.

The early texts do not discuss the concept of God, but they do portray, in parable and metaphor, the interaction and the relationship between God and the world. God is actively involved with the world, seeking its good and the good of all its creatures. These images point to a universal God who is the ultimate reality underlying and sustaining the world.

One can raise the question of God in several ways. This chapter concentrates on only one way to raise the question; it asks if and how God can be consistently conceived. It explores the question of what can truthfully be said about God. The answers to such questions, admittedly, do not say all that there is to say about God in the Christian tradition. Indeed, such questions yield only the most broad and general outlines of a concept of God. Other dimensions of God's interaction with the world will be explored in chapters 5 and 6.

How can God be consistently conceived? What is the truth about God? The Christian tradition has described God in a whole host of ways. For example, God has been described in anthropomorphic terms (father), in zoomorphic terms (mother eagle), in terms of inanimate objects (rock of our salvation), in terms of perfection surpassing all human language or taking all human characteristics to their ultimate possibilities (omnipotent, omniscient). Descriptions of God are not necessarily all consistent with one another or even, perhaps, internally coherent. Yet, when Christians speak of God, they understand themselves to be telling the truth about what is the case concerning reality. They understand themselves to be making claims about the structure of the universe. To discuss with others with different views of how reality is to be conceived and of what in reality is ultimate demands clarity from Christians. It behooves Christians to know what they claim about God and how they might justify such claims. The truth of Christian claims about

God is more often assumed than justified by believers. So any serious exploration of God or conflicting claims about ultimate realities must deal with the question of truth. As Keith Ward says, "Metaphysics is not what saves us; for Christians, the act of God, establishing creatures in knowledge and love of him does that. But metaphysics is needed to set out the coherence of the concept of a God who can so act in a world like this."[2]

What Is Truth?

Supposedly universal "truth" is today recognized to be interwoven with the interests of particular privileged groups. Thus a "truth" that is supposedly disinterested, holding equally for all, has worked to the advantage of a particular class or race or nation or gender. Images of the sovereignty of God, for instance, must of course be evaluated on the basis of whether they adequately represent the God-world relationship. But they must also be seriously scrutinized for whether they grant credence to a social structure wherein a person or a few people or a group is given consistent and comprehensive power over the lives of many. Conceptions of God that have claimed philosophical adequacy, and therefore truth, have still often been, without any forethought given to their impact, expressed in terms of male language. Thus a supposedly universal expression of truth carries with it the baggage of patriarchy. Those who have been disadvantaged by supposedly universal claims have rightly come to be suspicious of them.

The sheer diversity of claims to truth and the fact that they cannot all be easily reconciled to one another have also led to rethinking the concept of truth. That "truth" is so contested has led some to argue that it is not the world but the notion of truth that is problematic. Proposed solutions to this dilemma vary. Some propose that all truth is contextual, that any and all claims to truth can only be made within a given community where certain basic commitments are shared. Worlds are social constructions. In such cases claims to truth are, in essence, statements of shared worldview. Another position claims that the distinction between true and false is not appropriate. For this position, truth is not a matter of noncontradiction: truths can and do contradict one another yet can be simultaneously held. Yet another option holds that decisions about what to believe are not decisions about truth, but decisions made for pragmatic reasons. Another view would posit that "truth" is not a matter of making true claims. Rather, it is a matter of how well one's life is lived. We shall look at variations of these positions.

Gordon Kaufman argues that Christian faith is one "worldview" or "particular, relative and limited" perspective that has developed in history:[3]

> To acknowledge forthrightly and regularly that our theological statements and claims are simply *ours*—that they are the product of our own human study and reflection, and of the spontaneity and creativity of our own human powers and imaginatively envision a world and our human place within that world—is to set us free from these all too easy but false moves toward authoritarianism, which has characterized so much Christian theology in the past.[4]

In the current interreligious context, recognizing the imaginatively constructive nature of all religious traditions should propel us toward serious discussions with those of other traditions. The question of truth is not raised directly except to say that no tradition possesses absolute truth. Christian theology is a hermeneutical and constructive enterprise inquiring into fundamental Christian categories and reconstructing them to serve the contemporary worldview. Kaufman does not dispense with assessment, however, for he does argue that Christian theology needs to be judged according to whether or not it has been "destructive, damaging, or oppressive to humans, and thus evil" or has promoted human fulfillment; and whether its formulations are "archaic and misleading" or "provide adequate, full and insightful understanding of our contemporary existence, its problems and possibilities."[5]

Both Paul Knitter and Leonard Swidler speak of truth as "relational." Knitter objects to a notion of truth defined by the principle of noncontradiction. He argues that truth must be defined "not by exclusion but by relation."[6] According to Knitter, each religion contains some unique truth, but it also partakes of "absolute truth." "The more the truth of my religion opens me to others, the more I can affirm it as absolute."[7] Truth is defined in terms of openness to others. The more open a religion, apparently, the more true it is. Knitter offers three criteria for determining the truth of a religious tradition:

The Christian God and Truth

1) *Personally*, does the revelation of the religion or religious figure, the story, the myth, the message–move the human heart? Does it stir one's feelings, the depths of one's unconscious? 2) *Intellectually*, does the revelation also satisfy and expand the mind? Is it intellectually coherent? Does it broaden one's horizons of understanding? 3) *Practically*, does the message promote the psychological health of individuals, their sense of value, purpose and freedom? Especially, does it promote the welfare, the liberation, of all peoples, integrating individual persons and nations into a larger community?[8]

Knitter does allude to "divine truth" but does not clarify how relational truth is connected to it.[9]

Swidler speaks of the "partial, perspectival, deabsolutized nature of all truth statements."[10] One may be describing the same reality as one's neighbor and one may describe that reality truthfully, but it could be truthfully described by others in other ways from other perspectives.

Both Masao Abe and Raimon Panikkar eschew views of truth that adhere strictly to the principle of noncontradiction. Abe affirms a "positionless position" of acknowledging no common denominator among religious traditions. Although Emptiness is the ultimate ground of religious traditions, this Emptiness is dynamic and formless, "free from any standpoint."[11] Truth is not a matter of *either* this *or* that. "Since 'Boundless Openness' or 'Formless Emptiness' is a dynamic activity of ever-self-emptying and thus is a positionless position which makes other positions possible and alive in a dynamic harmony, it cannot be imperialistic."[12] Panikkar claims that truth is not plural but "pluralistic."[13] "Pluralism affirms neither that the truth is one nor that it is many."[14]

Religions, according to Panikkar, have true but unique and mutually incommensurable insights. Reality is pluralistic and transcends our ability to think about it. It is not reducible to any monolithic unity. Truth is constituted by the total relation of things to one another, a relation we can never fully grasp. Yet Panikkar also speaks of a "true religion" as one that delivers the promised goods to its members by achieving existential truth and honest consistency and that presents a view of reality capable of sustaining intelligent criticism from outside without substantial contradictions.[15]

Langdon Gilkey opts for a pragmatic approach to questions

of truth. There is no philosophical or religious way to come to a universal standpoint because both philosophy and religion are relative culturally, historically, and in other ways. Yet we all stand somewhere. Religious traditions are relative manifestations of absolute meaning.[16] One's own tradition takes on a "relative absoluteness."[17] To adhere to it is a pragmatic choice, giving one ground on which to stand. But one must also face the realization that this ground is not absolute. "Thus each particular religion is *true* and yet *relative*, a true revelation for that community, relative to other true revelations to other communities, and relative to the Absolute that each only partially and so somewhat distortedly manifests."[18]

Wilfred Cantwell Smith sees the category of "truth" more broadly than simply truth as a property of propositions. For him, religious truth is a matter of fostering life as lived. Religious life is not static, but fluid, bound to history. But Smith does not downplay the cognitive or intellectual dimension of truth. He maintains that no statement about a group's religious faith "is valid that cannot be appropriated by those persons."[19] Conversely, the honest person who is not of the faith group in question must also be able to recognize and accept the statements of those from within the faith group. Statements "first of all...must satisfy the non-participant, and satisfy all the most exacting requirements of rational inquiry and intellectual rigor. They must be more than objectively true; not less."[20] Smith is not a relativist in the sense that he regards all religious ways of life to be equally "true." For him truth is eternal and in life lived historically we can only approximate it.[21]

The positions outlined above evince widespread disagreement about what truth is and how to evaluate it. But they advance important concerns by acknowledging that claims to truth have been influenced by historical and sociopolitical factors. Such circumstances make attractive views of truth that lay no claim to universality. A truth that does not claim universality cannot ground such positions as religious imperialism or patriarchy, positions that are rightly seen as problematic today.

Although abandoning universal claims solves some problems, others, even more difficult, arise. Adherents of various religious traditions do not understand themselves to be merely stating a point of view but to be telling the truth about the world and their involvement in it. Although universal claims to truth have in certain instances led to lording one religious tradition imperialistically over others, if religious traditions make no claims to truth beyond themselves they become trivial. As merely innocuous expressions of one point of view alongside another, they would carry no power or depth to invite or command participation. Reasons for adhering to a religious tradition would not include that it told the truth about the way the world and its inhabitants are. One would speak of something as true because one believed it, rather than of believing because it was true. Roger Trigg poses the problem as follows:

> When confronted with religious disagreement, it may be very tempting to give up claims to objective truth, truth that holds for everyone whether they recognize it or not. It seems more tolerant and humble to say that even if something is true for us, it may not be true for everybody. Truth, however, then depends on the fact of belief. I no longer can believe something because it appears true. It is now true, for me, because I believe it. The result is the kind of fideism which rejects the idea that what I have faith in has any independent existence. My faith in God is thus not faith *in* anything or anybody. It must be a fact about me. Questions of objective truth must return if faith in God implied that God somehow existed independently of my faith.[22]

Religious traditions are unquestionably historical, and their concepts and claims are products of their social and cultural milieus. But to acknowledge the contextuality of religious traditions does not readily answer the question whether they are totally and without remainder socially constructed. Unless something that could be called reality can be distinguished from (if not totally separated from) our interpretations or social constructions of it, we are doomed to live in solipsistic "communities" of one, bound finally by our own individual experiences. Even if whole communities were to agree to see things in certain ways or to act in certain ways, nothing could connect them to other communities who saw things differently or who chose different courses of action.

If there exists nothing but our constructions of the world, then all religious belief is fideism and can be comforting or "meaningful" only until its lack of foundation is exposed. Further, neither could injunctions to activity, to ways of being in the world, claim universality. Although one may welcome this absence of universal claims when purportedly universal claims are patriarchal or imperialistic, giving up all thought of universality also abandons the possibility of argument against such positions in the name of more worthy claims. As Gregory Baum notes, the postmodern turn to relativism is not helpful for liberation theologies:

> While liberation theology laments the dominance of instrumental reason in contemporary society, it does not reject the entire Enlightenment tradition: it still trusts the critical methods capable of uncovering the extent to which economic and other forms of domination are reflected in the realms of ideas, culture and religion. Liberation theology resists the postmodern proposal that these theories must be rejected because they make universal claims.[23]

The next chapter more fully explores the possibility of universal claims to justice. It suffices here only to note that the rejection of claims to universality entails more than the rejection of claims concerning the truth or falsity of statements.

Rejection of any notion that religious beliefs claim to tell the truth about the way things actually are not only means that one's own beliefs are trivialized. It also removes any need or reason to take another's religious tradition seriously. Why grapple with another's religious claims if her or his way of construing the world is seen to be making claims only about him or her, not about the world at all? Although it would seem on the face of it tolerant, charitable, and fair to say that all religious traditions are equal and equally express something about their adherents, such a tactic does not seem nearly as charitable when one sees that it implies that one's conversation partners from another religious tradition are simply misguided or wrong if they think they are making claims about the nature of reality.

Courses of action, valuations, beliefs can clash. They can be incompatible with one another such that one cannot hold to two such opposing courses of action, valuations, or beliefs without absurdity. One may have to unpack what is involved in seemingly conflicting beliefs (for example) to be sure that they truly are in conflict. If one is to claim, as this chapter will, that "God exists" is a true statement about reality, about the way things are, then nontheistic ways of construing the universe are wrong. In making such a statement as "God exists," however, one must be clear about just what the referent of the term

The Christian God and Truth

God is and about what sorts of theism might or might not be supported by argumentation. Then one must see in what ways such arguments clash with arguments for a nontheistic construal of the universe. But, finally, if one is clear about what is in dispute, one cannot claim both that God exists and that the universe should be conceived nontheistically.

To call something true is to say that it is worthy of being believed, that it merits or warrants general acceptance. It is to say that reasons can be adduced to support the thought or conviction expressed. Because claims to truth are not all of the same logical type, various sorts of claims to truth require different sorts of argumentation. To argue for the truth of a claim is to determine what sort of claim is being made and to seek to adduce or provide the best possible reasons for it.

One of the complications in current discussions about truth in religion is that offering reasons for a claim has sometimes been artificially severed both from the actions that such a claim has been or might be used to justify and from its affective dimensions. The context in which the claim is made does have an effect on the credibility of that claim. In other words, truth has often been not only distinguished but also separated from goodness and beauty. To separate arguments for truth from the context of the use of those arguments is to foster the notion that truth has little relation to life as lived. Sometimes, in a desire to overcome the ideological freight of particular positions, or in a desire to privilege individual experience, the idea of any truth but individual truths has been abandoned. As I have tried to show, the price to be paid for such a position is high.

Reality Is One

When Christians make claims about God they are making claims about how one should construe reality. They are also making claims about themselves, about what it means to be human in relation to God. Indeed, in many of the discussions of truth above, the second of these two issues becomes paramount. As long as I am somehow grasped by or drawn into a religious tradition, as long as it somehow becomes meaningful in my life, it is often assumed, I have dealt fully with the question of truth.

Religious traditions do have a central and irreplaceable existential dimension. A religious tradition seeks to illumine one's life as a participant in it. It seeks to draw one into its sphere. It seeks to provide one with meaning. But one justifies or evaluates the meaning provided partly by evaluating warrants for possible construals of reality and of what it means to be human. We shall now look in more detail at the first of these.

Currently there is certainly great skepticism, if not outright denial, of the possibility of universal claims among philosophers and theologians who have been affected by postmodernism. It is not difficult to see why. Many claims that purport to be universal are thinly disguised apologies for one version of domination or another. Appeals to human experience have been discovered to leave large portions of humanity out of account. Feminists began to appeal to women's experience only to be forced to recognize that it, too, was more diverse than unified. Thus wariness with regard to universal claims is certainly warranted. But must wariness translate into outright denial of the possibilities of all universal claims?

Arguments against making universal claims are of two sorts. One variety argues that there is no one reality to which all such claims can appeal. Reality is not one but many. The second type of argument allows that reality is one, but our constructions of it are so many and diverse, so contextually and culturally informed, that there is no way to know which, if any, construals of that reality are more accurate than others.

If reality is not one, then nothing can prevent the fragmentation of human beings into solipsistic worlds of one. Shared interests and shared community find no grounding. Sanity and insanity are finally just sharing in different but equally acceptable realities. Since no language would have referents beyond itself, language would describe no common reality, communication would at the very best be a matter of accident and, at the very worst, impossible. How can one understand another if there is no common basis, nothing commonly shared by or through which the other can be understood?

Human thought and imagination, human interests and obsessions interpret and construct the world. We learn to see the world, its events, and our connections with it in particular ways. At points we come to see that those interpretations or constructions are not the only possible views. They are among many competing views. We come to see that ways of seeing the world are not all alike, nor are they neutral. Views of reality

The Christian God and Truth

might well be to the advantage of some and to the disadvantage of others. It makes a difference to lives in the world who gets to say what is so and on what basis. It is not just a matter of one human being describing his or her reality and saying to others, "That's how I see things, you may see them differently." For the way one person sees things does affect others, does affect not only how others are permitted to see, but also how others are permitted to live their lives. My view of reality impinges on others' views. To live in this world is to be a social creature, one whose decisions and freedoms make an impact on the decisions and freedoms of others.

How we construe the world makes a difference to ourselves and others. Unless we are going to argue that the power to construe reality gives the right to construe reality, which in turn provides a construal of reality all should accept, we need to give serious thought to the bases on which we can argue. Unless all social constructions of reality are equivalent (an idea that most oppressed persons would dispute), on what grounds can one argue for the adequacy of some interpretations over others? It is precisely at this point that one cannot give up the notion of universal claims entirely.

If reality is one, we need to seek ways to describe it, to talk about it, recognizing that even though we cannot separate ourselves from our history and from our sociocultural contexts there may be ways to account for varied and diverse interpretations that do not require that we abandon all universal claims.

John Hick proposes the unity of reality. Underlying all talk about God in theistic religious traditions, and talk about ultimacy in other religious traditions, is what Hick calls the Real. Hick distinguishes between the Real (noumenal Real) and our perceptions of the Real (phenomenal Real). To postulate a Real in and of itself is the best way to account for the data presented to us by religions.[24] According to Hick we do not have access to or knowledge of the Real itself (*an sich*) but only to reflected human experience, thought, and expression of it.[25] Our experience, thoughts, perceptions are influenced by our social, cultural, and historical locations; and therefore we do not all describe the Real in the same or even in similar ways. According to Hick all the ways of describing the Real are roughly equivalent:

> By [religious pluralism] I mean the view that the great world faiths embody different perceptions and conceptions of, and correspond-

ingly different responses to, the real or the ultimate from within the major variant cultural ways of being human; and that within each of them the transformation of human existence from self-centeredness to Reality-centeredness is manifestly taking place—and taking place so far as human observation can tell, to much the same extent. Thus the great religious traditions are to be regarded as alternative soteriological spaces within which, or ways along which, men and women can find salvation/liberation/fulfillment.[26]

But if, as Hick claims, we have no access to or knowledge of the Real as such, there is no way to know that the various descriptions of it are, first of all, descriptions of this Real, and not descriptions of something else entirely. Nor, secondly, is there any way to assess that all such descriptions are on a par with one another. Unless human experience is experience of this Real and not some other, as distinct from human interpretations of and expression of the Real, there is no basis for believing the Real to underlie all religious belief, as Hick claims. As Timothy R. Stinnett cogently points out, if Hick's argument about the Real is to carry weight, he has to account not just for its existence (what Hick calls the noumenal Real) and for human perceptions of it (the phenomenal Real) but also for the essence or character traits of this Real that would allow us to judge human characterizations of it as more or less apt.[27]

Hick rightly sees a problem in the various constructions of ultimate reality. He does not wish to give up the idea that there is one reality to which all religion is response. Religious traditions seek to describe the ultimate rather than the penultimate. Yet he does not wish to assert one view of the Real over against another for fear of being imperialistic. His solution presents certain problems.

Instead of concentrating on conflicting views of the Real, Hick prefers instead to focus on the lives and actions that issue from varying interpretations of the Real. In his article "On Grading Religions," Hick argues that the basic criterion for assessing religious traditions is "the extent to which they promote or hinder the great religious aims of salvation/liberation," that is, how far they make possible the "limitlessly better quality of human existence which comes about in the transition from self-centeredness to Reality-centeredness."[28] Although I agree with Hick that human response to the Real is crucial to grounding and assessing human religiosity (see especially chapter 5), the problems of an inaccessible and unknowable ultimate reality remain. There is no point in seeking to describe the Real if all descriptions are equally applicable and are equally inapplicable because there are no possible standards for deciding among descriptions. It does matter to religious believers what that reality is and how that reality relates to them. An inaccessible and unknowable ultimate reality might just as well be no reality at all.

Experience and Its Interpretations

If reality is one rather than many, this, at least, provides for the possibility of argumentation as to its structure and the interrelations of its component parts. In addition to seeing reality as one, Christians and other theists claim that reality is most accurately and consistently conceived as theistic.

On what bases might such a claim be sustained? Argument from a particular and privileged revelation will not suffice if the argument is expected to carry weight outside the Christian tradition. Two other types of argumentation are possible. One could argue that, consistently conceived, the concept of God implies the existence of God (this is usually called the ontological argument for the existence of God). One can also argue that there is universal human experience which is best accounted for by the existence of God.

Most talk about experience focuses on experiences, on the ways in which one's particular individual (or group) identity is formed by a variety of differing interactions with the rest of the world. As we reflect on our experiences, inevitably we *interpret* them. As feminists have had to discover, talk about "women's experience" is often contested by women who do not see their own experience accounted for in characterizations of "women's experience." In light of the fact that any accounting of collective experience is likely to bring forth protests from those who do not see themselves in the accounting, many have shied away not only from all claims of universal human experience but from all claims of collective experience as well.

Can one's experience be distinguished from one's interpretation of it, or is interpretation all that there is? Especially for those whose interpretations of experience have been so long given by others, and who are just now learning the power of naming for themselves, it is tempting to say that naming or interpreting one's experience is the whole. Is it a sufficient account of experience if I as a woman working in two male-dominated institutions, university and church, say I do not experience oppression, therefore I am not oppressed? It would be possible, even likely, that others of my female colleagues would try to point out to me the illusory nature not of my experience but of how I have chosen to interpret it. "Does your experience really warrant the interpretation you have given it?" they would ask. The implication is that one interpretation of experience is more adequate than another not just on the basis of presumed ideological commitment but on the basis of the situation being interpreted. If such a situation and such a question are plausible, then experience is distinguishable from interpretations of experience.

So while John Hick argues that there is one noumenal ultimate reality that gives rise to a host of phenomenal experiences of that inaccessible and unknowable Real, I argue that because one can and ought to distinguish between experience and its interpretations, common experience of ultimate reality—which, as will become clear below, is given in all our experience—can and does give rise to a variety of interpretations. Such a view sees experience of ultimate reality as universal, and it recognizes a host of ways of articulating that experience. It does not require, as Hick's view does, that all interpretations of that experience be seen as equally adequate interpretations of an inaccessible noumenal Real.

We are accustomed to the fragmentation of experience. We treat experiences as discrete cognitive interpretations of various aspects of our dealings with what is beyond our mental selves. In this common view, experience is, in essence, a mental operation of interpretation. It is an operation that separates us from others, both human and nonhuman. My experience is mine alone and sets me apart. If experience is nothing unless it is named by the experiencer, only those creatures capable of interpreting and articulating experience can be said to experience. Such talk of experience also separates us from our bodies, for it assumes that the experience of the body is nothing until it is cognitively interpreted by the mind. In such a view, experience is only experience when it is reflected on and articulated. Thus, for example, when we have talked about women naming their experiences, we have talked about how women have interpreted for themselves and others what has occurred to and around them.

Alfred North Whitehead, on the contrary, proposes that both sense experience and knowledge (interpreted experience) are derivative rather than primary. According to Whitehead, underlying experience as reflected upon or analyzed into specific categories lies what he called nonsensuous experience of the whole. Such experience is dim, barely conscious. It does not perceive discrete parts but is an impression of the whole. Before we analyze experience into particular constituents, we experience the whole of that to which we are connected and ourselves as part of that undergirding whole. "This is primarily a dim division. The sense of totality obscures the analysis into self and others."[29] According to Whitehead, the details add definition to the totality, not vice versa. We do not add up the details to come up with a whole, we focus on the details as part of an already given totality. No matter how comprehensively we try to list all the details that make something the totality that it is, such a comprehensive description fails, in part because we might leave out some descriptive detail that might interest someone else examining the same thing and in part because there is more to the whole than simply the sum of constituent parts.

One can point to glimpses of primary experience. When we come upon a place for the first time we get, before discriminating into details, an overall impression of the place, a sense of the whole and its relation to us. We sometimes talk of "intuition," and by this we mean a total disposition toward a person or state of affairs before analyzing our response into discrete and "rational" reasons. Children must be taught discriminations of color, shape, and sound; that is, they must be taught which discriminations are counted as important in their own sociocultural environments. If sensory experience were primary, then one would expect these discriminations to be given with the experience itself. When we first awake, we receive an overall impression of our surroundings rather than one which is separated into clear and distinct images and patterns. We do not experience our bodies or our own immediate past through our senses but through nonsensuous experience. Nonsensuous experience is presupposed by analysis of experience into its details or cogni-

tive reflection interpreting experience as experience of something or other. Primary nonsensuous experience characterizes
or underlies any experience or state of affairs. According to
Whitehead, primary experience is experience of value, a "vague
grasp of reality, dissecting it into a threefold scheme, namely,
'The Whole,' 'That Other,' and 'This-My-Self.'"[30]

Whitehead's notion of primary experience makes sense to me.
Although all experiencing is also experiencing of the particular,
which then can be analyzed into constituent elements different
from the constituent elements of some other experience, the intimations of primary experience as undergirding experience of
myself in relation to the other, and the whole as experience of
value or worth, ring true. "We are, each of us, one among others;
and all of us are embraced in the unity of the whole."[31]

Primary nonsensuous experience is characterized by integrity, interconnection, and value. We experience the whole
rather than its parts. We experience ourselves as part of rather
than separated from the totality, as one among many. Worth or
intrinsic importance is the affective dimension of nonsensuous
experience. "Have a care, here is something that matters!"[32] I
am suggesting that experience of *integrity, interconnection,* and
worth underlies all experiencing.

The integrity, interconnection, and value of reality are often
lost to us when we begin to concentrate on the parts and details.
But, as we are beginning to rediscover from the ecological movement, for example, we lose sight of these three characteristics of
experience to our peril. The ecological movement has pointed us
again to the interconnectedness of the world. The herbicide we
spray to kill "weeds" washes into the water table and is ingested by
a variety of animal and plant life until it comes back to us in our
food. The fact that we have failed to recognize the intrinsic value
of some species has meant that they have become extinct through
the human notion that things are only valuable instrumentally as
humans put them to use. If we fail to recognize the wholeness, the
totality, we consider large portions of it simply expendable.

Feminists also have lauded the characteristics that I have
here portrayed as common to all experience. Many women are
seeking an integrity, a wholeness, that they find lacking in
their day-to-day dealings with the world. Yet the intimation of
wholeness, though elusive, is there to hope for, to strive
toward. Feminists have sought to reclaim their connectedness

77

to one another and to the rest of the world. There has been much feminist writing about relationship[33] and about the far-reaching implications (social, political, and ecological) of words and actions that have previously presented themselves as having totally predictable and limited consequences. The notion, for example, that "the personal is political" presents well one dimension of the interconnectedness of existence. If a woman is battered in her own home, this is not an isolated act of "private" violence but is connected to a much broader web of social and political relationships.

Women's intimations of their own intrinsic worth have led to raised consciousness about who we are as women in relation to ourselves and others. These intimations of intrinsic worth also raise feminist awareness of their interconnections with all that is and of their search for the integrity of all, not just "isolated" parts.

Because we are so used to attending to the differences among experiences, we rarely seek the unities. But if White-head is correct, as I believe he is, that clear and distinct experience, and thereby also individually interpreted experiences whose interpretations are influenced by a variety of factors, are narrowing from more general, indeed universal, human experience of integrity, connectedness, and value, then reality must be such as to give rise to such primary experience:

> When we survey nature and think however flitting and superficial has been the animal enjoyment of its wonders, and when we realize how incapable the separate cells and pulsations of each flower are of enjoying the total effect—then our sense of the value of the details for the totality dawns upon our consciousness. This is the intuition of holiness, the intuition of the sacred, which is at the foundation of all religion. In every advancing civilization this sense of sacredness has found vigorous expression. It tends to retire into a recessive factor in experience, as each phase of civilization enters upon its decay.[34]

The foundation of religious life is not a wide variety of experiences of the phenomenal Real, as Hick would maintain. It is, rather, our primary experience of the integrity, connectedness, and value of reality. Religious differences arise, to be sure, and they are real and important differences. They arise, I would argue, from differing interpretations of primary nonsensuous experience.

The task for one who would espouse one interpretation of nonsensuous experience rather than another is to show how an interpretation best fits that experience. Our primary experience is not one of the value of discrete and separate things but of the value of the whole. I would argue that nonsensuous experience of a valuable whole is best interpreted by positing an ultimate reality capable of valuing the whole as a whole. Granted, entities within the universe can value one another. But the limitations of contingent existence, limitations of space and time, mean that some existents, no matter how intrinsically valuable, will never be valued in actuality by other contingent existents. And, also given the limitations of contingent existence, limited beings can value only parts of the whole and not the whole in itself. Yet our intimations of value suggest value of the whole. Unless there is a valuer of the whole, what "the whole" becomes is simply the sum of its parts. If the whole is the sum of the parts, the primary experience of integrity is counteracted. As a limited and contingent being one is connected only to a small number of the other entities in the whole. Yet one's primary experience intimates the connectedness of all things. Experience is most fully accounted for by an ultimate reality, experienced in all nonsensuous experience of the whole, which is the matrix of the universe. Here this reality will be called the deity or God.

The argument is this. The value of the universe as a whole requires one to value it as whole, as well as in its parts. The integrity of the whole requires one who is its integrating principle. The interconnectedness of the whole requires one in and through whom all is connected. As I will suggest below, the dipolar theism of Charles Hartshorne offers a God who both transcends and includes the world, one who as personal being can and does value the whole and who as being-itself also includes the whole. Our primary nonsensuous experience of value, interconnectedness, integrity is also experience of God who underlies, connects, and gives value to the whole. As primary experience, our experience of what I am here naming God is not analyzed, reflected on, or classified as such. Our primary experience of God is not of God *as God*—that requires the kind of cognitive reflection that has here been called knowledge. One can experience what I am here naming God without ever articulating that experience as experience of God. What I am calling primary experience, including experience of God, comes to us in our specific historical, cultural, and social locations. That I am arguing for common experience does not mean that one gives up the specificities and particularities of experience. We neither have nor reflect on experience in a vacuum. Thus, one could, of course, analyze and name differently that to which I am pointing as common experience. Our specific experiences and interpretations of the world in which we live and our location in it give rise to the language and conventions of interpretation. The language and conventions of interpretation we inherit in our own context give rise to particular ways of seeing or analysis. This is not a closed circle, however, for there is not mere repetition, but also modification.

Let me hasten to make a few clarifications. Not just any "God" will do. That is to say, conceptions of God within Christianity and other theistic traditions are many and varied and often contradict one another. Thus, to argue that the universe is most adequately conceived as theistic does not mean that every conception of God is equally adequate. A fuller description of God remains to be worked out.

Also, this argument will undoubtedly be disputed at many points. Although I think I have given an accounting of universal human experience in speaking of what I, following Whitehead, am calling primary or nonsensuous experience, others might well dispute its universality. The main point to be made here is that counterarguments need to take seriously the possibility that experience is not fully accounted for by beginning with interpreted experiences, such as sense experience and knowledge. Second, to argue from primary experience to a theistic conception of the universe might be countered by others who think this experience is better accounted for by other construals of reality. John Cobb argues that religious traditions might well not be in conflict in describing reality. Rather, they may simply be attending to different aspects of reality. He suggests that "God" answers a question about why there is an ordered world at all. "Emptiness" answers a question about what one is and what all things are.[35] It is certainly possible that by some construals of both concepts, God and Emptiness are not incompatible. If they do answer different "ultimate" questions, one would have to examine clearly how the answers to these so-called ultimate questions were, ultimately, related to one another.

In the argument being advanced here—which draws on onto-logical, cosmological, moral, and design arguments for God—what is meant by God is the universal one who both undergirds and transcends the world, giving it value and integrity by valu-ing and integrating it.[36] Theism appears to me the most ade-quate way to account for the value of the whole because God as individual (yet universal individual) is its valuer.

Deity who undergirds all must be one whose existence is not contingent. God, in order to be God, is not one who might cease to be. As Charles Hartshorne rightly notes, one does not talk of the existence of God in the same terms as one speaks of the existence of other individuals. One does not say God might or might not exist, as one might speak of a tree or a person. The options are, rather, that God exists necessarily or the concept of God makes no sense; that is, there is no consistent conception of God. If God can be consistently conceived, God exists. (This is called the ontological proof for the existence of God.)

If God values the universe, God must be one to whom the universe makes a difference. Traditional views of God have often seen God as absolute, as one which nothing can affect or change. Hartshorne makes the perceptive point that God is one to whose bare existence nothing can make a difference (that is, God exists necessarily) but that God is also one to whom all that happens makes a difference. God is not defined by static perfections, but by unsurpassability. Although God cannot be surpassed by any other existent, Hartshorne argues that God can be surpassed by Godself in terms of integrating into Godself new relationships and new values. God can integrate into Godself all the novelty brought about by creaturely choic-es. God does not foreknow our choices but reacts to them by integrating the value they create into Godself. God is supreme-ly absolute in terms of characteristics that do not admit of addition of value; such characteristics are abstract and include God's existence, infallibility, and worshipfulness. No matter what, God exists, knows what there is to know, and is worthy of worship. But God is also supremely relative, in relationship with all that exists. All that is affects God, and God affects all that is. Whereas any given creature only interacts with a limit-ed number of other creatures, God interacts with all. How God exercises God's infallibility, for example, is contingent. God knows creatures as they are, and God's knowledge is affected by creaturely actions.[37] Although God knows all creaturely possibilities, God only knows what choices creatures actually make as the creatures make those choices. Thus, God integrates the novel into Godself and responds accordingly.

Whereas traditional views of God have stressed God's absoluteness and seen relativity as inimical to a static view of perfection, Hartshorne's dipolar theism argues that relatedness to all is in itself a perfection, and what is more, a defining characteristic of a consistent conception of God. "There seems no contradiction in holding that in the transcendent being the essential core of identity is infallibly secure, while the peripheral content is responsive to every item of reality."[38]

Our primary experience of the interconnectedness of all that is points toward God not as separate from the universe but as including the universe. This concept of God is called panentheism. It is often confused with pantheism, the position that says that God and the universe are one. But the view of God drawn from primary experience points beyond the sum total of the parts of the universe to one who is capable of valuing the whole, one who transcends the sum total of the parts. Yet, if the one is the matrix of all that exists, then one might say, as panentheism does, that God includes the world. God transcends the world while including it. To say that God includes the world is to say that God is in intimate relation with the world so that God takes all that is into account. All that is contributes to God. Sometimes this inclusive relationship is likened to the relationship between mind and body[39] or spirit and body[40] or to the relationship between a pregnant woman and the developing fetus.[41] The biblical image of God is also one of relationship and interaction. God is seen as one who responds to creaturely activity. The biblical God does not only act but also reacts.

Describing God

Even if I am correct about primary experience, it is clear that the interpretive mechanisms and language available to one for characterizing primary experience are always laden with historical and sociocultural baggage—for instance, the term *God* and the masculine pronoun *he.* Although Whitehead and Hartshorne purport to be formulating strictly philosophical concepts of deity, they still, without any particular thought given to the matter, call this deity *he.* Yet there is no reason, given the views of God that they hold, that this pronoun should be used. They take up the ideological baggage of a male God alongside their purportedly neutral philosophical views. Indeed, some feminists would argue that even to use the word *God* indicates maleness, given that the English language also offers the possibility of *Goddess.* But the word *God* is not necessarily a male word. For example, the existence of the words *actress* or *poetess* does not imply that *actor* or *poet* are necessarily or exclusively male words. *Deity* does not capture the notion that the one indicated is *a* being as well as being-itself, although the deity would do. *God/ess* (Rosemary Radford Ruether's term) or *G-d* (Elisabeth Schüssler Fiorenza's suggestion) are also possible. In monotheistic traditions, despite the male baggage that has often accrued to the concept of God, the traditions themselves have strongly upheld the notion that God is not a sexual being. Because I think that one can infuse non-male content and imagery into the term *God,* I continue to use it. I am not, however, unmindful that in using it one must always counter its patriarchal associations.

One must be mindful that universal claims are always embedded in historical and sociocultural contexts and proclaimed in language that brings its own baggage along with it. Thus, claims about universal human experience are spoken and heard in particular times and places. One needs always to be attuned to how claims about the universal are being used, for they may well be appropriated to foster less-than-universal benefits. No matter what arguments one makes for the universality of God, if this purportedly universal God is used to argue for the favorable treatment of some as opposed to others, then one is pushed back to look at the purportedly universal concept again. Claims to truth are easily co-opted. One must be constantly wary and vigilant.

My discussion of God has yielded the barest description. Any further elaboration on who God is depends on a number of factors. Once we have recognized that our images of God are in part the result of our experience of God and in part the result of our social and historical location, one must look again at scripture and tradition. One must consider what images of God are central to the tradition. One must come to some determination of their status. Are these images essential to the way Christians speak of God? One must look at these images in light of what has been claimed here to arise in universal experience.

In light of primary experience of God, no attribution of gender to God is suggested or fitting. The one who is universal individual does not have a gendered body, thus any gendered language can only be symbolic or metaphorical. The Christian scriptures and tradition agree that God is not a gendered being. Yet scripture uses, for the most part, male pronouns and images of God. The image of father is one of these. Father imagery is not nearly as prevalent in the Hebrew Bible as it is in the New Testament. It is often claimed that Christians are bound to use the term *father* for God because Jesus revealed that as God's name.[42] But, as Elizabeth A. Johnson points out, the use of the term *father* in the gospels is by no means uniform:

> Word count shows that God is referred to as father in the Gospels with increasing frequency: 4 times in Mark, 15 in Luke, 49 in Matthew, and 109 in John. More precisely, the frequency with which Jesus calls God Father breaks down even more dramatically: Mark 1, Q 1, special Luke 2, special Matthew 1, John 73.[43]

It would seem that the term *father* is used with increasing frequency in the early church rather than being given as the preferred and only proper name for God. In addition, even if Jesus does call God father, surely this term indicates far more about relationship than it does about the exclusive use of the term father for God.

If *father* is used exclusively as God's name, then, intentionally or not, one gets the impression that God is male, for our use of the term *father* is invariably for males. Then one needs to ask about the sociocultural implications of imaging God as male. Although by themselves male images of God might not translate directly into patriarchal structures, if one examines the interaction between male images of God and social structures one can see that male images of God can bolster patriarchy. If divine authority is connected to male authority, women lose out. It happens as simply and easily as the Sunday school child who says: "Women can't be ministers because God's a man." It happens with a vengeance when men claim for themselves the power and right of God to batter their wives. It happens when little girls cannot see themselves included in either the social milieu or the religious universe.

Such an argument does not necessarily imply that one needs to abandon entirely the image of God as father. Indeed, there are ways in which the image of fatherhood attached to the concepts of integrity and interconnection suggested above might itself be a counter to traditional images of fatherhood. The caution here is against using exclusively images from one sex, thus infusing that sex with connection to the divine. The caution here is also against so deifying one human image that it becomes an idol, taking the place of the God it is supposed to name.

For the argument of this book the major point to be made is this: God is not male, and any discussions of God in interreligious contexts need to be very clear about this. God is the one who undergirds all that is, who values the whole and gives it value, who connects and integrates the whole, and who fosters integrity and interconnection. This description, while true, is also sketchy or skeletal. It provides only the bare bones. If they are to live, then we also need symbol or metaphor to give a richness and depth to our language about God. We need to find images that can evoke response. But we also need to find images that do not oppress or give warrant for the imperialistic superiority of one group over others.

The biblical tradition can be the source of some such images. The Bible contains stories of an interactive God of love who rejoices when creatures rejoice and weeps when they weep. Yet, as the discussion about the maleness of God shows, not all biblical images are usable or useful. The biblical images need to be read critically through a variety of lenses, including the lens of the God here discerned through primary experience and the lens of feminist critiques and those of other oppressed people and groups.

We can also build up images and metaphors for God from contemporary experience or other religious traditions, provided they are consonant with the basic values and concepts argued here to be central both to primary experience and Christian tradition.

The usefulness of images and metaphors for God is situation-variable.[44] Images that can be understood and used in some contexts may not be useful at all in other contexts, perhaps because of their historic associations, or their potential for use as oppressive tools. Referring to God solely in male language may have spoken differently to other times and places than it does to us today. Images of God as shepherd lose their immediacy in a society where very few people keep sheep.

The ultimate reality described here and named God or the deity is not one inimical to feminist aims. God is one who imparts value and fosters integrity and interconnectedness. This God does not foster dualisms of superordination and subordination. If reality is as described here, its hallmark is not fragmentation but integrity for all beings. God is not beyond the world and unaffected by it but its matrix, the one who is affected by all that happens. God is not the stern and judgmental punisher but the one who is supremely relative to all that is. God does not coerce events in the world but responds to the free acts of creatures in a mutually creative universe. This God does not serve patriarchy.

As reluctant as some feminists are to appear intolerant by claiming truth for their positions, the alternative presents serious problems. If "truth" is just "true for me," then it is difficult to see on what foundations a feminist case for social change could be made. If truth is totally perspectival, then claims to justice find no basis in reality for there is no reality in which to base them.

Sheila Greeve Davaney suggests that feminist theology, and indeed feminist theory more generally, should give up "the appeal to ontological reality as a grounds of validation for our positions."[45] Davaney argues that only such a position as her own takes the historical conditionedness of all positions and all knowledge into full consideration. Carol P. Christ agrees that truth is relative, but according to Christ, not all truths are equal: "Commitment to feminism does not have the same ontological status as commitment to patriarchalism."[46] Feminist experience gives the lie to thoroughgoing relativism. Christ sees thoroughgoing relativism as in itself a pretense to a detached neutrality. The diversity of women and of women's experiences means that they will not all interpret reality in the same way. Reality is in large measure socially constructed. What is interpreted in one way can often be interpreted in many ways. But unless those social constructions are totally rootless and random, not just any construction of reality is possible. This chapter has explored in detail only claims about the intersection of experience and interpretation of ultimate reality, but other claims about reality will be explored in the next two chapters.

Differing Accounts of Reality

In this chapter I have argued that religious traditions make truth claims, and, in particular, make claims about the nature of reality and what about reality might be said to be ultimate. I have set forth a theistic account of ultimate reality, arguing that, as I see it, this account is most adequate. Clearly this is not an uncontroversial or uncontroverted claim. One whose view of ultimate reality is quite different might well make a different argument and a different set of claims to adequacy.

The door is not shut to different accounts but opened to them. In giving reasons for a theistic view of reality, I have not discounted the possibility of other reasons for other views. One might well seek to base quite different interpretations of reality on what is here called primary experience. Once differing interpretations are given to reality, these interpretations take on sociocultural and historical lives of their own. Thus, when we interpret our primary experience, we interpret it from within a given context. For instance, that I account for the ultimate in reality as *God* and not as *x* is shaped in part by the linguistic convention of the Jewish and Christian traditions that name personal ultimate reality as *God*. I continue to use this term as I function in a Christian context. But neither the name nor the interpretation is itself the reality of the ultimate of which we are here speaking. One could disagree with my account of experience. One might agree with the account of experience but interpret that experience in such a way as to come to a different view of what ultimate reality is and how it should be described, arguing, for example, that a nontheistic or a polytheistic view better fits experience. One could conceivably decide to name the ultimate reality described here in a brand-new way to eliminate all former concepts and confusions and thereby constitute a new religious tradition. What I hope I have done is to set up a position that is open to genuine discussion. If John Cobb is correct that various religious traditions answer different ultimate questions and thus describe different aspects of ultimate reality, one would have to show how those questions relate to one another, and to the overall structure of reality. Thus, someone from another religious tradition might well construct a different argument about reality or ultimate reality. I would hope that another such construction would offer a variety of possible points of contact as I have sought to offer here. To offer such points of contact does not mean that one would come to consensus or agreement. It does mean, however, that one would come to know as clearly as possible what is at stake in the differences.

Accounts of ultimate reality are not the only aspect of religious traditions. They are always intertwined with accounts of how one should respond to that ultimate reality. In the case of the description here, why should one respond to this God? How should one respond to this God? If this chapter does tell the truth about God, then, of course, it is well to take the truth seriously. But the barest description of God does lack a certain visceral quality. Universal truth describes experience, to be sure, but it does not describe experience in all its richness, fullness, and complexity.

Theology does well if it tells the truth about God, but in terms of the relationship between God and human beings something more is needed. Here is where the question of God becomes not only a question of truth but also of human response and the creation of a relationship between particular human beings and God. Further, it becomes a question of the valuation of the whole. If the whole has value and God is the valuer, how does everything, not only human life, attain to the greatest possible value in response to the one who values? In what ways does the world contribute to the one who values it?

The discernment of truth can rightly be claimed to be a value for God. But there are other values as well. As we have noted, the ideological distortion of truth has led to injustice and the exploitation of others. Other values are needed alongside truth to help guard against its distortion and exploitation by the interests of groups. Human response to God can take many forms. In the next chapter we discuss how the value of goodness is or is not embodied in human responses to God. Knowing the truth may not always lead to doing the good, so goodness and its connection to truth must be examined.

To know the truth and to do the good still might be said to leave out the dimension of feeling, of existential enjoyment. Human response to God has taken other forms than morally good activities or their opposite. Production of value should not be limited to moral activity. The fullest satisfaction of entities also includes the production and experience of beauty.

5
Human Response
and the Good

The Christian tradition answers the question, "From whom shall we obtain fullness of life?" by pointing to God. It answers the question, "Through whom should we live?" by indicating Jesus Christ. But this leaves unanswered the question of what fullness of life entails.

The Christian response to God through Jesus Christ is a response of faith, of trust. The experience is not one of hearing truth claims expressed in general, but one of being directly and personally addressed. The experience of value that was articulated in the previous chapter takes on a historical and symbolic context, it is "re-presented" to Christians in Jesus Christ. This direct and personal address transforms one's life. Just as Jesus enacts the reign of God, the Christian response of faith is enacted in Christian life.

The response evoked by God through Jesus Christ is one of proclamation and action, proclamation of an experience of encounter with God through Jesus Christ and action toward the neighbor. The message of Jesus is a message of reconciliation with the other, of love for one's enemies, of receiving and offering for-giveness. It is a message of urgency for the reign of God. It is a message that emphasizes that actions speak louder than words. It respects none of the traditional social orderings—putting the last first, caring for social outcasts, placing faith claims above family relationships, reversing the order of master and servant, taking women as seriously as men. Love of God and love of neighbor are placed side by side. As J. D. Crossan puts it, one is drawn into unmediated contact with God and with others.[1] The end in view is fullness of life.

The Biblical Message of Fullness of Life

The message is all the more necessary and powerful because fullness of life was denied for many in Jesus' time, as it is in ours. In the Christian tradition, the human predicament is diagnosed as one of sin or fall. Despite the possibility of recognizing and building on our connectedness, in their freedom and finitude human beings are alienated from God, one another, and the rest of the world. This alienation has issued in sinful acts toward others. In the Christian tradition this is linked to the "original" sin of Adam and Eve. Whether all evils in the world are linked to human sin has been a matter of debate in the Christian tradition over the centuries. The point to be made here is that humanity finds itself not in an ideal state but one in which fullness of life is in many ways impossible for many.

The earliest layer of the gospel tradition does not discriminate among persons as to their sex, social class, ethnic origin, family status, and so on. Yet clearly also the biblical writers were not immune to upholding the interests of certain social groups. Perhaps in Paul, certainly in his redactors and in the writers of the pastoral epistles, men are valued more highly than women, seen as more like God and more appropriate church leaders.[2] No great programs for the reorganization of society came out of the early church; for example, slavery was not condemned. Responses to Jesus were easily channeled into ideologically acceptable forms.

Yet if we examine the relationships and responses evoked by Jesus' action and teaching, we find clues for human activity. The experience that the earliest followers had of Jesus was one of God's love or grace surrounding *them,* valuing *them,* counting them as important. As the biblical stories recount, Jesus diagnosed and responded to what he encountered. He had no one solution for every situation. What Jesus made present and evoked in others was an experience of grace, of wholeness, health, healing, love, fullness of existence. Response to Jesus did not take the form of obeying set rules but of seeking to communicate fullness of existence to others. Today we too should seek to provide for one another the conditions of that fullness of existence, although as we shall see, one's context plays a major role in determining exactly what conditions make for fullness of existence.

Just as varying images of and claims about God need to be subjected to critical scrutiny with a view to sorting among competing claims, claims about human moral activity also must be critically examined beyond the religious traditions in which they arise. We need to explore in what ways those who are not Christians might be able to relate to the injunctions to action drawn from Christian tradition. In addition, one must also explore more concretely what it might mean to live the moral life today.

Judging Religion by Moral Claims

John Hick, as we have seen, argues that the basic criterion for judging the adequacy of religious traditions is a moral criterion, "the extent to which they [religious traditions] promote or hinder the great religious aim of salvation/liberation. And by salvation or liberation I suggest that we should mean the realization of that limitlessly better quality of human existence which comes about in the transition from self-centeredness to Reality-centeredness."[3] By a better quality of human existence, Hick means that which promotes the well-being of individual and community. While he recognizes that there have been many cultural variations in interpreting such a criterion, and in deciding who actually belongs to the community in question, he sees a basic moral consensus in promoting welfare and avoiding harm.

Paul Knitter also proposes that one of the criteria for evaluating what he calls "the truth value" of religious traditions is a practical or moral one: "Does the message promote the psychological health of individuals, their sense of value, purpose, freedom? Especially does it promote the welfare, the liberation of all peoples, integrating individual persons and nations into a larger community?"[4] He opines that religious traditions can find common ground in the search for liberation from oppressions, where one would take up a preferential option for the oppressed.[5] He suggests the need for liberation from physical suffering, from socioeconomic oppression, from nuclear danger, and from ecological disaster as "'the common human experience' painfully present to all

Human Response and the Good

religions."[6] Such a common ground is not an absolute, but a heuristic device:

> Still, by applying the criteria of liberative praxis, by asking, for example, how a particular Hindu belief or Christian ritual or Buddhist practice promotes human welfare and leads to the removal of poverty and to the promotion of liberation, we might be able to arrive at communal judgments concerning what is true or false, or what is preferable, among different religious claims or practices.[7]

Yet Knitter maintains that particular understandings of liberation are provided by specific individual religious traditions. He is wary that his suggestions for liberation as a common center for religious traditions might be seen as an argument for a common foundation; he wants to "propose," not "impose."[8] In his work, Knitter argues that orthodoxy should be subordinated to orthopraxis.

Drawing on feminist and liberation theologies, Marjorie Suchocki proposes that justice be the criterion by which religious traditions are judged. Although she recognizes that justice has culturally bound interpretations and instantiations, she rejects the notion that this calls for relativism and argues that the criterion of justice transcends our particularity.[9] By justice, Suchocki means "inclusiveness of well-being," an inclusiveness opposed to all ideology that distorts knowledge and sets up exploitative relationships.[10] Suchocki sees three levels of justice: physical well-being, human dignity and recognition in the human community, and openness to self-development and self-determination.[11] "The ultimate test of justice is precisely the degree to which it knows no boundaries to well-being."[12] To cope with the variances in interpretation of justice within the world religions, "we must look to the heart of justice in each religion as that which renders life meaningful in light of a vision of what existence should be."[13] Because Suchocki is wary of how religions tend to become ideologies, of how adherents of one religion tend to see themselves as superior to adherents of other traditions, no one religion's vision of justice will suffice. Yet, to keep justice itself from being an imperialistic norm, "the determinate mode of justice must be drawn from the vision of the termination of adversity or the ideal form of human existence envisioned in each religion."[14]

Suchocki, Knitter, and Hick all see the way in which human beings act or are enjoined to act as central to a judgment on the adequacy of religious traditions. They all hold the opinion that religious communities might well be able to come to common cause in areas where activity is required more easily than they can agree on questions about the structure and symbolization of reality. We are entering into a discussion of "the good," by which, here, I will mean the moral good, that which is worthy of being done. As with discussions of truth, discussions of the morally good can be carried on in general terms or in a concrete context. Today such discussions are almost always carried on with a particular and specific context or issue in view because it is rightly recognized that general discussions leave too open the possibility that particular actions will be easily ideologized and rationalized. Yet to leave the general discussion aside completely is to risk not noticing the interconnections between varieties of activities or between activities and values.

Moral claims must be sustainable in the face of opposition to them. If, as a woman, I claim that I have a moral right to the goods and values of society, I must have some idea of what those goods and values are and why I should not be deprived of them or given them in lesser proportion than males are. If someone from a so-called developing nation claims a moral right to a portion of the world's goods to keep herself and her brothers and sisters from starvation and disease, her claim implies that moral goodness should be extended beyond national or racial boundaries. If these claims and others like them are not to be rebuffed by arguing that the claims are simply perspectival reversals of their opposites, that those who earn the goods deserve to keep them, then some basis for moral claims must be sought.

Specific religious traditions have provided grounding for their own moral claims. In the Christian case, the first and most direct appeal is to the Christian tradition and to the love of neighbor authorized by it. Love of neighbor in Christian tradition is grounded in the love of God for the world. But if one is not a Christian, why should one accept the Christian teachings about activity? In addition, Christian claims about the specifics of "love" have often been in conflict.

Knitter does not seek to justify the claims he makes for the centrality of liberation beyond the observation that many religious traditions seem to be able to endorse such a view. Hick maintains that the moral claims of religious traditions are related to the various views of "Reality." But, as we saw in the previous chapter, according to Hick, there is no way to justify the various phenomenal views of Reality as more or less accurate representations of that Reality. Neither can activity be so justified. For Suchocki, it appears that justice or inclusiveness of well-being is a concept held or insisted on universally enough to be its own justification.

Who has a moral claim on another is a question often decided by naming a group to which both claimant and other belong. Yet the very naming of such a group is rife with the possibility of ideological exploitation. Who is in the group and who out? What are the criteria for inclusion? Who gets to decide? Talking about "common humanity" glosses over differences that are often not even noted.[15] And, in an age when ecological disasters and nuclear holocaust are ever possible, is "common humanity" a sufficiently broad category by which to name moral claimants?

Some would argue that there are no ways to ground ethics. The radical historicity and diversity of particular existence and experience makes any common ground for activity as impossible as common ground for belief. Others have taken radical diversity and historicity seriously but seek to ground human conduct in the historical lives of others, for example, saints.[16]

Recognition of historicity and diversity reminds us that no conceivable grounding for ethical activity can exist or be implemented apart from a serious consideration of the particularities of any given context. Yet, as Seyla Benhabib argues cogently, universalisms should not be dismissed. They should be rethought in light of the criticisms of feminism, communitarianism, and postmodernism.[17] Benhabib portrays a universalism that takes seriously historical consciousness and the concrete other. She grounds her universalism in a conversational model of rationality, wherein a "willingness to reason from the others' point of view" is central.[18] She does not think that one can attain consensus, but one can attain mutual comprehension of points of view and build on that. She argues for a universalism that is not committed to "the metaphysical illusions of the Enlightenment,"[19] to self-transparent and self-grounding reason, to a disembedded and disembodied subject, to an Archimedean standpoint beyond contingency.

Like Benhabib, I seek a universalism that takes historical particularity and embodiment seriously. I do not think that all metaphysics either can or must be abandoned, if by metaphysics we mean an appeal to general statements about reality, but I do think one must be much more modest about what metaphysical claims can be made and more realistic about how such claims are affected by the concrete and the particular. If metaphysics is possible, it must be a metaphysics that does not dismiss the importance of difference on the way to grand theories of belief and action.

The experience of value, integrity, and interconnection to which I made appeal in the previous chapter is also, I would argue, the basis of moral claims. The parts of the universe (whether at the micro or the macro level) have value in and of themselves and contribute value to one another and to the whole. To be is to have value. Nothing has merely instrumental value for someone else. All that is has intrinsic value. If the universe has integrity, then the scope of value must be the whole and all its parts, not just some arbitrarily chosen portion. If the universe is one interconnected whole, then what happens to the individual parts affects other parts as well as the whole. When human beings take seriously and act on their primary experience of value, they seek to create value in response.

To talk about the morally good is to talk about the possibility of creating values for the self and for others with whom one shares the world. It is to talk about creating situations that allow for the maximum flourishing of existence. Human beings are beings of freedom. They see choices open before them and can act on some possibilities and exclude others. Human beings can reflect on their activities. They can analyze the situations in which they find themselves and can think ahead to the probable consequences of their activities. More than any other creatures of which we are aware, human beings can be held responsible for their choices, for they can foresee many of the outcomes of their acts, and the effects these acts will have on others.

I do not wish to argue that all human beings are faced with identical choices, or that all have the same capacity to effect change. Below I will discuss a variety of constraints on human freedom. What I do wish to suggest is that it is within human capacity to act in ways to facilitate maximum flourishing of the self and others, or to act in ways that inhibit the flourishing of self and others.

To say that to act for the good is to create the conditions for the maximum value for the self and others and, therefore, for God, the valuer of the whole, is not for a moment meant to deny the difficulties in determining the specifics of such activity. Nor is it intended to downplay the immediately apparent reality that far too many people act with individual self-interest or the self-interest of a very restricted group in mind.

Human Response and the Good

From the various manifestations of the ecological crisis we have learned that the contemporary anthropocentric view of the world and the good has been far too restricted in its scope. We are having our primary experience of interconnections to the rest of creation reinforced in starkly concrete ways. Plants and animals, for example, have value for themselves and for God, not only for humans. In the next chapter we will explore beauty as a value to which all parts of the universe contribute. In this chapter we will concentrate on the category of the good, which, in terms of the actual creation of values, is more anthropocentric and more limited than beauty.

The very interconnectedness of all that exists means that sorting out competing interests is difficult. To say that everything has value is not to provide a criterion to adjudicate among values. But it does provide scope for thinking. The interconnection of all that is means that the creation of value is in the interrelationships among existents. The actions of one are responded to by another; neither act is predictable. Thus, context is all-important.

Because of the social nature of the universe, its parts do not and cannot act as isolated individuals. Freedom to act for its own well-being might well bring one part of the whole into conflict with another. There are incompatible courses of action that clash and must be resolved. At the level of human conduct, human beings are faced constantly with decisions about how to balance their own desires, or the desires of a particular group, over against other desires and values. In the human case, activity is complicated; although capable of reflection beyond themselves and, thus, of foreseeing some of the consequences of actions, humans often ignore the vast implications of their decision making. They ignore the full scope of vision. To act only in one's own narrow interest or in the interest of a small group is a mark of alienation from the whole. In the Christian tradition this alienation is termed *sin*.

Human decision making takes place, as it were, in medias res. There is no place beyond to stand and act. The decisions made by others before one and prior decisions in one's own life form the context in which one's own decision making is possible. Certain things are simply "givens," for example, our past histories and the histories of others or our bodily characteristics and limitations. Yet our context today is also formed by historical consciousness. We recognize that our social structures are humanly created and, however much they come to seem like the very fabric of reality itself, can be humanly changed. Within the broad matrix of inter-connection, we have created our own patterns of social relations.

To concentrate on the maximizing of value is not as utilitarian in orientation as it might first appear. Maximizing value is not creating maximum good for the maximum number as though some existents could be easily sacrificed on the way to a total good. In the schema proposed here, the whole only attains value as the parts contribute to it. And each part has and creates value to contribute. Thus what is needed is always a recognition of the common interests of part and whole. A contribution of value to the maximal value of the whole must always be considered within its context, and with each existent's value recognized.

The view proposed here also is one that takes embodiment seri-
ously. One might talk about value in the abstract. But the creation of value and benefiting from value creation require concrete embodied beings. Value is actualized for particular beings in specific historical situations. In particular, moral value is only value *as enacted*. Talking about moral value does not create such value.

Concrete Questions about Maximizing Value

Questions of the morally good first arise in the concrete. They arise as people begin to question how some are treated at the hands of others. Although I have suggested a general approach to these questions in terms of maximizing value, the actual working out of what that might mean must take account of the context in which the questions arise and in which they can be answered.

The notion of maximizing value is easily ideologized, particularly if one ignores the universal scope of moral claims. It is tempting to view as important only the maximizing of value for oneself or for a small group, rather than for the whole. Patterns of social interaction, once created, take on a character of permanence. In the Western world until the Enlightenment, God was seen as the prime creator of social organization. Even after we recognize that patterns of relationship are humanly constructed, however, dominant social patterns are viewed as unchangeable and justifications for retaining them as the only acceptable patterns arise. Those who benefit most often begin to arrogate to themselves that they are the ones who properly "count" and that they "deserve" what they have "worked for." Those who benefit most often begin to see themselves as the central and final recipients of value.

Feminist analysis begins with the experience and observation that in patriarchal societies men have more access to what a society takes to be important, whether that be food, money, power, range of life choices, political and ritual roles, or status. Feminists raise questions about the relative valuing of men and women. They ask why men are seen as the normative and women as the derivative form of humanity. They seek social and political changes that would give women access to the ranges of goods and choices men have, as well as changes in the patterns of thought that undergird and support male dominance. As feminist analysis has proceeded, it has become clear that more than just a question of gender is at stake in determining women's access to the goods and values of society. Class and ethnic background, geographic location, religious affiliation, sexual orientation, and many other factors influence the places women occupy in sociocultural relationships. Difference has often become a matter of superordination and subordination, rather than a matter of welcome diversity.

Marjorie Suchocki's three levels of justice are useful here as a way to understand the maximizing of value. Her analysis recognizes that actualizing justice is dependent on the context in which the claims arise. Also, she does not put personal values and social values into separate spheres as if one did not influence the other. She suggests physical well-being as fundamental; then comes the ability for self-naming and appreciation of self and others in the human community; third is the possibility of self-development and self-determination within the context of the communal good.[20] Although we continuously try to overlook or to ignore it, the physical overabundance to which some have access is connected to the physical lack of others. To maximize value is not to hoard physical goods but to distribute them widely. The wider distribution of physical goods will enable the creation of value for the whole at other levels as more human beings have the time and energy to live their lives beyond mere survival.

Physical well-being also includes the possibility of living one's life without constant threat of its being taken by another. In many parts of the world humans live in constant danger of violent death. Women in most societies of the world live with the fear of rape and death at the hands of men. That even in North America we do so little to stem the high incidence of violence perpetrated against women by family members results from our failure to grasp the *scope* of value. We prefer to see matters in which we are not directly involved as not our problem and ourselves as not part of the problem. We separate private and public spheres and profess no responsibility for the "private" sphere of another. Yet, if we are honest with ourselves, the interconnection and integrity of the whole pushes us to begin thinking differently.

In terms of self-naming and self-determination, and allowing the possibility of the same for others, Suchocki's categories impel us to recognize further implications of moral activity. Although physical needs are central and crucial, full human lives require more than full stomachs. Human beings need to be able to develop their skills and potential as fully as possible and to gain satisfaction from that development. As individuals and groups, human beings need to be able to determine the values in their own lives and ways of meeting those. For such development to take place, appropriate individual and communal conditions have to prevail. Thus moral activity has political and communal as well as individual venues and implications. If one views moral or ethical activity as basically activity by and for individuals, one misses the larger social and political context. This view fails to take account of the interconnectedness of individuals as parts of the whole. It also fails to take into account human responsibility for creating and upholding the social and political contexts in which we live our lives. Here, the feminist slogan "the personal is political" is well remembered. Former ages may have assumed political and social contexts simply to be "givens." But by studying varying contexts through history and geography we know that the actual form and structure of social and political relationships are humanly created and can be humanly altered. In showing how we need to change our view of "good works" beyond the individual to the political, a Canadian social reformer from the early part of this century, Nellie McClung, makes the following point about the parable of the Good Samaritan:

> The road from Jerusalem to Jericho is here, and now. Women have played the good Samaritan for a long time, and they have found many a one beaten and robbed on the road of life. They are still doing it, but the conviction is growing on them that it would be much better to go out and clean up the road![21]

For women, maximizing value means access to the physical means of existence. But it also means recognition of women as full and equal human beings and as participants in decision making and creation of meaning at all levels. Each context demands specific attention to the changes needed to maximize value for women, and although the formal analysis presented here cannot, by itself, answer the question of what is needed in each situation, it does provide a framework for feminist decision making.

Suchocki's analysis also needs broader scope. Her analysis, useful though it is, is largely anthropocentric. She directs her attention to justice for human beings. But the value, interconnection, and integrity of the whole should impel us to yet broader analysis. If humans are not the ultimate determiners or recipients of value, and if, to put it theistically, everything that is contributes value to God's experience of the whole (as will be argued more fully in the next chapter), then the scope of human moral activities needs to be broader than just humanity.

Our responsibility in our own activity to maximize the creation of value in others extends to animal and plant life, indeed to the whole planet and beyond. Through human activity we have removed values created by whole species of animals and plants. We have assumed that accumulating value for *some* humans is more important than the distinctive value created by a whole species. Like humans, other animals and plants are contingent beings. Individuals come into existence and die. The continued existence of some individuals depends on using other individuals as food. Even if all human beings become vegetarians, they will need to destroy plant life in order to survive. There is no possibility of retaining all life just as it is. Yet, large-scale destruction of life, both plant and animal life, needs to be a matter of great concern, as does viewing such life as only instrumentally valuable, valuable for human use. We do not maximize value when we pollute the seas, killing marine plants and animals, not for food but as a by-product of acquisitiveness and accumulation. We do not maximize value when we clear-cut forests, destroying all that we do not want to use and removing habitat for wildlife in the name of "economic" values that are frankly and merely anthropocentric and accrue in large measure to a very few human beings.

The scope of value that I am suggesting is vast and is, admittedly, complex, especially since we have ignored this scope for a long time in the name of the creation of surfeits of values for limited numbers of human beings. Thus, we, in medias res, have a very long way to go to make changes that would value the world differently. Liberation movements in the world have much to say to the current world situation. Liberation theologies push us to take a "preferential option" for the poor, for women, and for the environment. These preferential options would not be needed if the scope of human responsibility had been better balanced in the past. Liberation thinkers argue that only a dramatic shift of priorities will counteract the prevailing narrowness of value-creation. Christian liberation thinkers maintain further that God also exercises preferential options for the downtrodden.

The Christian tradition, if we take seriously its claims about God and responsibility to God in our present contexts, not only contains resources to foster the creation of values now mooted but also ought to foster values-creation for individuals in the context of the whole. It has often fallen short of this potential, however, because it has been co-opted and ideologized. Feminists have shown how women have often been subordinated and marginalized in Christianity, both in terms of their actual access to a wide variety of roles available to men and in terms of the ways in which church teachings have created and maintained views of women that have led to their continued subordination to men in church and society. No amount of claiming that ordination has nothing to do with human rights and that women have different but equal roles will blunt the criticism that the major positions of power and privilege in many churches are simply not open to women. If a church gives mostly men the right to make ethical pronouncements, especially about issues such as birth control and abortion, which primarily affect women, it has not allowed half its population to name their own experience or to engage in a process of self-determination. The point to be made here is that under the guise of moral good, the church has often limited the serious discussions that must take place when questions of the maximizing of value are under consideration and, under pretense of neutrality, has constricted the scope of fullness of existence for its female members. Rules have triumphed over relationship, abstract pronouncement over concrete context. Further, the rules themselves have not been examined in terms of their own ideological limitations. Who had a say in their formulation? Whose interests do they serve? Do they maintain privilege for some at the expense of others? For whom are values being created and for whom restricted? If privilege for some is masquerading as the good of the whole, unanalyzed ideology triumphs.

Women who have found meaning within the Christian church

Human Response and the Good

have also experienced oppression within that same church. Women have raised serious questions about the gap between the articulated scope of church ethical claims and the actual experiences of women in the church and in society as a result of church teachings. As we shall see below, this gap and all gaps between ideal and practice become important in a religiously plural situation.

Common Action across Religious Lines

The world's religious traditions in their distinctive ways call into question precisely this placing of ultimate value in the self or in the small group. If an individual or small group is not seen as ultimate, then whatever is seen as ultimate calls for response to the ultimate and places the individual or group into context. Importantly for interreligious relationships, even though religious traditions may disagree about how to characterize and symbolize what is taken to be ultimate, the nonultimacy of human individuals or small groups focuses the moral good broadly rather than narrowly.

When one combines a broad view of who and what ought to be included as claimants to the moral good with a recognition of certain common and pervasive moral problems besetting the world today, one might well be able to come up with common approaches and proposed solutions that cut across religious lines. Although religious traditions cannot be confused with or equated with moral activity, pressing world problems are crucial issues for most religious traditions since their views of reality have implications for activity.

When diverse religious groups can agree on common activity to meet moral claims, it opens the doorway for further communication and understanding. Interreligious groups have been able to agree on and enter into such projects as feeding the hungry and to craft joint positions about how to eradicate poverty. Many world religious traditions have been able to enter into work together for peace and justice, both in global and in particular ways. Although it has been argued here that primary human experience of value, integrity, and interrelation functions as a foundation for human moral activity, it is not necessary to agree on or to articulate a common basis to enter together into a common act. One may engage in common activity from a variety of motivations and goals. One hopes, however, that religious traditions do try to articulate reasons for the activities in which they engage, reasons that speak to outsiders as well as to insiders of the tradition.

Common activity and discussion informing common activity are yet another level on which interreligious interaction can take place. Each religious tradition articulates its motivations for such common activity or the symbolic structures fostering such activity differently. But when bonds of common action can be formed, no one religious tradition can claim moral superiority over others. Adherents of religious traditions begin to realize that although persons might act out of Christian or Jewish or Buddhist motivation, the act itself is not exclusively a "Christian" or "Jewish" or "Buddhist" activity. Morally justifiable activity is not the province of any single religious group.

When comparing the moral stances of religious traditions one has to be aware of the great gulf that often develops between a tradition's moral ideals and the actual practices of its adherents. Adherents of any religious tradition need to be constantly self-critical. They need constantly to listen to the moral claims posed for them both from within and from outside the tradition to recognize the gaps in their own practice. Ideological self-delusion needs constantly to be challenged by self-critical honesty. As mentioned in chapter 2, women from various religious traditions need to get together and make coordinated moral claims in light of each tradition's own professed ideals.

Truth and Goodness Are Connected

Religious symbol systems embody what a religious tradition takes to be ultimate. One of the central criticisms of religious belief and activity today is that their justifications are disembodied and abstract. Religious symbols function precisely to make particular ways of belief and action concrete. Yet concrete symbols can also be co-opted for ideological purposes. Human activity can be ideologized in such a way that it benefits certain individuals or groups and disadvantages others. Further, justifications for moral activity on the part of religious individuals and groups are often drawn from what can be highly ideologized symbol systems or interpretations of reality. In other words, truth and goodness are intimately connected. When the scope of claims to value is narrowed, whatever is conceived of as ultimate often begins to be assigned the characteristics of the dominant group. The social structures of earthly society become the prototypes for the social structures of "heaven," as it were. When we ignore or forget that the language that we use of the ultimate is human and grows out of particular social contexts and social relationships, we are tempted to think that our language for the ultimate is given by the ultimate itself. For instance, describing God as King grows out of a particular period in the history of Israel; but if this is not recognized, monarchical language for God can become normative for describing God's relation to the world as well as undergirding patterns of human relationship with one "ruler" and many "ruled."

We need always to examine the historical and social contexts in which religious images and symbols arise to understand the function of the images in their original contexts. We need to look at the implications such images had for action in their original contexts. Who, if anyone, was advantaged by the use of particular sets of images for the ultimate? Who, if anyone, was disadvantaged? What happens when particular images are transferred to the current context? Who benefits? Who loses? The relationship between religious symbols and human activity is not a straightforward one of cause and effect. Yet, insofar as religious groups appeal to their views of ultimate reality to ground ethical claims, a clear and close relationship exists between descriptions of ultimacy and of activity deemed appropriate in response.

Speaking of God in male language, for example, may not in and of itself be responsible for patriarchy. But if male language for God grows up in an already patriarchal context, if male language is seen to describe God more accurately than female or impersonal language, if male language is seen as God's "real" name rather than as metaphorical description, then male language for God will provide a powerful symbolic reinforcement for male superordination.

On certain understandings of reality one can foist responsibility onto reality itself for the creation of social relationships, thus absolving dominant groups from responsibility for changing inequitable states of affairs. On the understanding of reality presented here, the matrix is given in which relationships among creatures take place but within that matrix human beings are responsible for the social structuring and naming of their interrelationships. In addition, humans have created the social structures that precede and surround us. Thus, although there are givens and constraints, some physical and some ideational, on our relationships, most of these are humanly created and can be humanly altered.

How reality is named, then, is crucial to the pursuit of goodness as well as to the pursuit of truth. If the pursuit of goodness, of maximum creation of moral value, is to be attained, it matters how reality is named. Statements about reality, thus, can and should be judged not only on how adequately they describe reality, but also on the sorts of activity they foster.

The Good and the Beautiful

Because of the pressing moral claims in our world today, it is tempting to see religious traditions only in terms of how well they deal with moral issues. Future possibilities for the world and its inhabitants clearly depend on how well humanity meets current global crises such as hunger, ecological disasters, poverty, and war. Yet human life is not accounted for in its totality by understanding human ethical activity. Humans are involved in many pursuits that do not easily fit into the category of the "good." Even many activities articulated as in direct response to religious experience are not simply or solely activities that can be seen as morally good or not good. Not only do people act for or against their neighbors, but they also create music, literature, art, rituals, and liturgies. And although such creations might well have influence on ethical acts (indeed, the next chapter will argue that they do), creation of moral goodness or value is not their primary or only purpose. Such creations enrich the lives of their creators and of others in a distinctive way.

Creation of the moral good is, among creatures, a human prerogative. But is moral good the only value to be sought? A cat or a flower cannot anticipate and act toward its future with the moral consequences of the act in view. Unless its value is only to be instrumental for human beings, valuable insofar as useful to us, the category of value needs to be broader.

In the next chapter I will suggest that, in addition to the values of truth and goodness, theology makes claims about beauty, and thus, Christian theology needs to begin to take seriously the category of beauty. I will also argue that taking beauty seriously offers yet one more important venue for interreligious understanding.

6

Fullness of Existence
and Beauty

Human response to God through Jesus Christ cannot be accounted for totally in terms of moral activity toward or on behalf of another. The Christian tradition has given rise to expressions of faith in art and music, architecture and literature, prayer and liturgy, and in numerous other ways. Although such forms of expression do have implications for moral activity, they are not primarily directed toward the moral good, nor toward propositional truth. Further, moral good done toward another enhances life and the possibility of fullness of existence for the other. The acts in question are creative of, expressive of, and evocative of value, value that will here be named "beauty."

When we read the earliest texts about human responses to Jesus, we pick out first the interactions that lead to the moral good. This is in part because of our current attunement to issues of justice. The biblical world made no distinction between what we now think of as moral and aesthetic. The effect of Jesus on others was not only a call to moral activity, but was also an effect that changed their whole lives. Jesus evoked affective or emotional as well as moral response from his hearers. Jesus evoked faith. He engaged others not just intellectually or morally but with the whole of their being. One of the criticisms made of Jesus was that unlike John the

Baptizer, who was an ascetic in matters of food, Jesus indulged in feasting. He fed his body rather than deprived it and invited others to share in his festive meals.

Engagement with the whole of one's being leads, in turn, to varied responses. Those who encountered Jesus told others about their experience in words as well as moral acts. They sought to evoke the experience they had had in others by their own proclamation. The early Christians inherited traditions of response from the synagogue, especially written texts, liturgical forms, hymns such as the Psalms, and special spaces for worship. Certainly very early, followers of Jesus developed their own forms of prayer and worship or took over available forms. Very early the acts of baptism and Last Supper became activities with symbolic and evocative import. (Although John Dominic Crossan, for example, sees neither the Lord's Prayer nor the Last Supper as part of the historical Jesus tradition, he does see them as early traditions.) Followers of Jesus combined stories about Jesus into complex literary texts. They wrote hymns such as that contained in Philippians 2. They enacted their faith not just in moral activity but in worship and proclamation.

Early Christian artifacts include murals in the catacombs and elaborately carved sarcophagi and a few church buildings. Much more art and architecture in the service of Christianity followed on Constantine's decision to make Christianity the official religion of the empire. Creations of words, music, art, and architecture were used to give glory to God and to call others to faith.

But the aesthetically pleasing is sometimes seen as a distraction to the real work of Christian believers. The ascetic tradition of the desert mothers and fathers, begun in the fourth century and carried on in parts of Christianity ever since, sees the need to keep the pleasures of the flesh under control. Food, sex, physical comfort are thought in this part of the tradition to get in the way of a truly spiritual life, which is envisioned as a life opposed to the life of the flesh. The ascetic tradition in Christianity tends to foster dualism, a separation of mind and spirit from body. It tends to see the body as a burden to be endured on the way to true spiritual life with God.[1] The aesthetically pleasing and the ascetically disciplined life are not necessarily opposed to one another. Ascetic discipline need not always signal a dualism of flesh against spirit; it might connote eschewing certain forms of experience for the cultivating of the fulfillment of experience in other ways. Nor must the aesthetically pleasing always signify self-indulgence. Enjoyment or fullness of existence is not necessarily a kind of rank hedonism that seeks pleasure without acknowledging the larger context in which one lives.

The earliest Christian tradition does not point to rigid submission to the will of another, even God. If the argument of this book has been correct, the Jesus of the earliest tradition portrays the truth about God and evokes a response on behalf of the neighbor; but also does something more. It seeks fullness of life not only for the neighbor, the other, but also for its hearers; it seeks to bring its hearers to wholeness, a wholeness of personhood broader in scope than right belief and action.

At many times in the Christian tradition it has been fashionable to contrast purportedly Christian love, *agape*, with other kinds of love, most particularly *philia* and *eros*. *Agape* is said to be selfless, disinterested, self-sacrificing for the other. And Jesus is seen to be the prime exemplar of *agape* whom all Christians should seek to emulate.

Yet the earliest texts about Jesus proclaim him not as one who was disinterested but as one supremely interested and involved. Early texts about Jesus portray his care and concern for fullness of life, not through a disinterested love but a relational one. In relations with one another, we can call forth fullness of life both for others and for ourselves. This love is closer to *eros* than to *agape*; it requires that we be involved in life, not stand at a distance. This love engages the whole person, not some distanced and distancing moral or intellectual judgment. It is enfleshed, embodied. In addition to fostering the true and doing the good, the Christian tradition points toward a further dimension of fullness of life, an aesthetic dimension, beauty.

Satisfaction of Experience

In addition to spelling out the claims christology makes about truth and goodness, therefore, we also need to look at its aesthetic implications. Entering into the realm of aesthetics, one finds, if it be possible, even less agreement than in spheres of intellectual and moral claims. This is partly because aesthetic theory has seemed to many to be esoteric at best and confined to the relatively narrow sphere of artistic creation or production. In the end, we have mostly been content to let judgments concerning the aesthetically pleasing rest individually with each creator or perceiver. This attitude appears in such prevalent ideas as "I don't know anything about art, but I know what I like" and "There's no disputing taste."

Human beings have always tried to create what is aesthetically pleasing. Beyond those things necessary for mere survival, they have always sought what would further enrich life. They have decorated functional pieces and created things whose central purpose was not functional. If we confine aesthetics to the realm of artistic production, however, we miss the connection of such production to the whole of human life and ultimately to the rest of existents.

Creation of the aesthetically pleasing is part and parcel of the desire to experience life satisfyingly or well, to experience life to its fullest.[2] Humans seek pleasure, joy, and satisfaction, in addition to their mere continued existence. And they find what they seek partly in creating works of beauty and enjoying such works created by others. Works of art, music, architecture, and literature enrich human experience. Our moral acts provide for enrichment in the lives of others. But not all that enriches human experience beyond mere existence is a human creation or production. Human experience is enriched and enlivened by experiences of other humans and of the natural world.

Beauty, aesthetic value in its most general terms, is what is worthy of being enjoyed. Beauty provides for the fullest enjoyment or enrichment of life. To experience fulfillment of existence is to experience beauty. Although beauty is more than affect, to talk of beauty takes us further into the realm of affect, of feeling, than does talk of truth or goodness. No one can experience for or as another. What one finds beautiful, another may find tawdry. The enrichment of experience that one person seeks may be overwhelming or terrifying to another. A wide range of experiences may be satisfying to any given individual; thus one can rarely say, "Only this experience and no other will enrich my life."

If discernment and experience of beauty are purely a matter of individual taste, then the satisfaction of experience is simply inexplicable. There could be no common judgments as to beauty. At first glance this does not seem problematic. Unlike discussions of moral activity, what contributes to the overall enrichment or fullness of an individual's experience does not at first seem to matter much to others. But if fullness of existence beyond mere bodily survival is the concern, we do well to reflect on it in general aesthetic terms. Although in our first experience of beauty affect is dominant over cognitive analysis, emotion and intellect need not be in conflict with one another. As Lorraine Code points out, emotional response is not to be equated with the unstable or erratic; sometimes emotion is reasonable. "Emotion and intellect are mutually constitutive and sustaining, rather than oppositional forces in the construction of knowledge."[3] What are the conditions of fullness of existence, of satisfaction of experience, of beauty?

Charles Hartshorne maintains that aesthetic value or beauty is most comprehensively understood in terms of a balance of harmony and intensity. Beauty is often linked to harmony, but too much harmony is boring and insipid, while too much intensity is chaos or pain:

> There are then two notions of minimal value, not one. Either the degree of contrast or the degree of integration may be barely sufficient. Beauty in the emphatic sense is a balance of unity and variety.[4]

No one proper balance of harmony and intensity exists for all creatures at all times, yet creatures each in their own way can appreciate harmony and intensity. Hartshorne holds that beauty, understood as a balance of harmony and intensity, is a universal. "I believe that the basic idea of beauty as integrated diversity and intensity of experience is metaphysical, valid for any possible state of reality."[5] Satisfaction of experience is only possible when harmony and intensity come into balance:

> For each level of complexity there is a balance of unity and diversity which is ideally satisfying. What we spontaneously call beautiful exhibits this balance. Discord, diversity not integrated by unifying factors, is not very good; but a too tame harmony or unity, not sufficiently diversified with contrasting aspects, is not very good either. And at the extreme limit, one form of aesthetic failure is as bad as the other; for in either case experience becomes impossible. To be bored to death is not better than to be shocked to death.[6]

One can create aesthetic value for oneself and others by providing for the possibility of experience that balances harmony and intensity. Such experience can be enriched through the human creation and enjoyment of works of art which are often centrally identified with the beautiful. But it can also be fostered through human contacts with one another and with the rest of the natural world and through more "mundane" experiences such as the aroma of baking bread or the feel of a silk scarf.

Aesthetic value, defined as the satisfaction of experience, or that which is worthy of enjoyment, involves the whole person. For example, to be engaged in the production of a great work of music, or to be fully engaged in the enjoyment of that same work, draws in my whole being. I am intellectually involved. But my primary intellectual involvement is not usually analytical when I am singing. I am physically involved in the production of sound. I am affectively involved, drawn fully into the music. In terms of the total experience, I do not separate these various involvements. The total experience is more than the sum of the parts. Some kinds of music strike me as insipid. They offer no challenge. They do not fully engage me. They do not contribute much to the satisfaction of experience because they are too boring or trivial. There is too much harmony and no intensity. Other kinds of music are so chaotic as to be barely music at all, they are collections of random and abrasive voices with no pattern, no melody, seemingly no harmony at all.

Aesthetic value is embodied value. Production of aesthetic value involves one in creating value for the self or another through the embodiment of value in the self or in the creation. It therefore contributes to the fullness of existence. Aesthetic value needs a medium, the medium of either the self or of its creation. In mediating aesthetic value, particularity is crucial. One does not experience "beauty" in general but particular embodiments of beauty, particular instances of beauty in their own historical and cultural contexts.

The same primary experience that grounds the production of moral values also grounds the production of aesthetic values. Our primary experience of value, integrity, and interconnection aids both our own enjoyment and in fostering enjoyment in others. Indeed, our primary experience is more closely aligned with the aesthetic dimension of experience than it is with the cognitive or moral dimensions of our existence. The value of the whole is felt or experienced as a whole before it is analyzed. We respond to value by seeking to create value, enjoyment, fullness of existence, for ourselves or another. Value created is not just value for the self, but for the whole of which it is an interconnected part. And, if my arguments in chapter 4 are accepted, value created is value created for God, the one whose scope allows for the valuation of the whole and all its parts.

There is a sense in which all life is an aesthetic process. To exist is to be creative, to take the past including one's own immediate past and, through the process of creativity, to contribute what one is to the future, to the self, to other existents, and to God. Charles Hartshorne speaks of the interplay and interrelationship of the whole of reality as a "drama" and calls this drama "the essential art."[7]

Beauty provides a depth dimension to experience. It grasps my whole being and it engages my whole self. It provides texture. Beauty allows for a variety of points of entry into any particular experience of the beautiful. No matter how much one plumbs its depths or engages in analysis, the element of self-creation through creating or experiencing the beautiful is finally an individual's own doing. Yet that self-creation is then offered to the whole and becomes part of the experience of others. In the same way in which courses of action might be incompatible with one another yet still all be moral, a range of experiences might be beautiful or contribute to fullness of existence. Still, individuals must choose some courses of action and therefore cannot choose others; they must choose some satisfactions of experience, therefore making others impossible. Analysis of beauty cannot in the end force individual enjoyment any more than analysis of action can force moral action. Yet the beauty in any individual's experience has consequences beyond itself.

Aesthetic Values Are Inclusive

Only human creatures, so far as we know, are capable of the forethought and planning required by moral activity. Human beings can enact moral value for themselves, for nonhuman creatures, and ultimately for God. But this does not mean that nonhuman creatures receive only the value granted them by humans and never create it themselves. Nonhuman creatures contribute to the value of others and to the whole by creating what is here called aesthetic value. Dogs, for example, can both relish the aesthetic values created by harmony and intensity in their own environments and contribute to the harmony and intensity of their environments. My dog, Holly, reacts to different kinds of weather in different ways. She glories in new-fallen snow, appreciating, perhaps, more of its aesthetic qualities than I myself, for I am content enough to look upon it to appreciate its beauty. Rarely do I focus on its smell and taste. She celebrates the differences in her daily routine in her own doggy way, and, although she appears less bored by the same routine day in, day out than I, she seems clearly to enjoy the contribution to her life that comes with a walk in the park where there are squirrels to rout and chase, and a variety of scents more diverse than those in her own backyard. She enriches my life with companionship and devotion, and with an element of humor. She contributes both harmony and intensity to the fabric of my life and the lives of those (including, perhaps, the squirrels?) with whom she interacts.

Charles Hartshorne maintains that aesthetic values are inclusive:

> Animals, including people, survive partly because they *want* and try to survive. This means, to put it simply, that living gives them pleasure, joy, satisfaction, or other aesthetic, that is, intrinsive values, and the thought (if they do think) of continuing to live gives them more of this value than the thought of not continuing. This holds whatever they may say or not say about it. Even moral values are intrinsically aesthetic to the extent that the sense of harmony with the good of others is an element in one's own aesthetic good, and that genuinely moral conduct favors aesthetic good in the future for others and, for the most part, for oneself. If living were not good in itself there would be no point in being ethical, or in anything.[8]

Nonhuman beings contribute value to one another, and not merely the instrumental value of one providing for another's survival. My dog enjoys the squirrels not, it would seem, because she views them as potential dinner, but because watching them and chasing them injects intensity into the harmony of her day.

Both human and nonhuman beings contribute value to God, the ultimate valuer. A lily, for instance, contributes its comely shape and its perfume to those around it. It may attract and enrich the lives of humans or bees, not just instrumentally but aesthetically. But the lily is not robbed of its value if no creature takes notice of it. It still contributes what it can to the whole and to the God who alone can value the whole for what it is. The existence of the lily adds value to God.

Beauty in Religious Tradition

In primary experience of value, interconnectedness, and integrity, the aesthetic dimension is dominant. Value, interconnection, integrity are felt qualities of life before they are cognitively analyzed or parsed into moral or intellectual implications.

Religious traditions have embodied primary experience in a wide variety of ways, many of them giving central place to the aesthetic dimension of fulfillment or satisfaction of experience. As Frank Burch Brown says: "Part of religious experience simply *is* a kind of artistic and aesthetic experience."[9] Religious traditions as particular concrete or embodied responses to primary experience involve the whole person or group; they impart, along with claims to truth and calls to action, felt qualities of primary experience.

In Alice Walker's *The Color Purple,* the following dialogue takes places between Shug and Celie.

> Listen, God love everything you love—and a mess of stuff you don't. But more than anything else, God love admiration.
>
> You saying God vain? I ast.
>
> Naw, she say. Not vain, just wanting to share a good thing. I think it pisses God off if you walk by the color purple in a field somewhere and don't notice it.
>
> What it do when it pissed off? I ast.
>
> Oh, it make something else. People think pleasing God is all God care about. But any fool living in the world can see it always trying to please us back.
>
> Yeah? I say.
>
> Yeah, she say. It always making little surprises and springing them on us when us least expect.
>
> You mean it want to be loved, just like the bible say.
>
> Yes, Celie, she say. Everything want to be loved. Us sing and dance, make faces and give flower bouquets, trying to be loved. You ever notice that trees do everything to git attention we do, except walk?[10]

In this discussion, Shug points to the mutual enrichment of God and humanity via aesthetic means. God wants us to delight in the aesthetically pleasing, in the color purple in a field or (in the discussion just previous in the novel) in the joy of sexual feeling. In turn, our enjoyment delights God (or, if we fail to notice, it "pisses God off"). Aesthetic enjoyment provided by God for the world and vice versa is part of what Shug calls "love," not a disinterested love that never seeks for itself, but a mutual relationship that is best described as eros, connection, real relatedness between God and the world. God is not equated with beauty, but the creation and enjoyment of beauty is one of the vehicles or means of mutuality of relationship between creatures and God. We sing and dance, make faces and give bouquets so as to provide enjoyment for others, to evoke relationship and love. And, according to Shug and Celie, both God and trees do the same. Walker provides a powerful accounting of the interconnection of all things in terms of the satisfaction of life they derive from one another.

The creation of beauty enriches both other individuals and the whole. And in the theistic view of the universe here presented, it also enriches God. In God's turn, God seeks for the universe the balance of harmony and intensity that will lead to maximum satisfaction of the whole and its parts. God evokes beauty.

In line with Hartshorne's notion of life as a drama, Frank Burch Brown points to the importance of viewing religious traditions as performance:

> Religion must be presented to and by the believer and devotee. Hence it must be *performed,* as it were, if it is to be perceived, received, or realized. The ongoing performance of a religion takes place in classic works and acts, as well as in non-classic modes; yet in a sense it is the religion itself that is the primary normative classic mediated in performance.[11]

An important part of virtually all religious life has been the ongoing enactment or performance of the tradition in ritualized ways. Although the purposes of ritual include telling the truth about the nature of reality and inspiring certain kinds of moral conduct, ritual speaks to the whole person in a way that, perhaps, a philosophical or ethical treatise does not. Ritual involves us bodily as well as intellectually in religious life. It might involve song, movement, story, or repeated formulaic words. It often retells or reenacts events central to the religious community. Participants are drawn into ritual in a variety of dimensions.

In Christian churches, and in other religious settings that include singing, we do not sing only to espouse certain doctrinal content or moral messages. The singing itself, the act of singing and hearing, draws us in and transports us beyond ourselves. We do not necessarily need to be singing or hearing song in a language we know to be deeply affected by it. Good music (we shall return to the question of taste later) evokes the enjoyment that is here called the aesthetic dimension of religious tradition and of life. It can also be a vehicle wherein, as we are drawn beyond ourselves, we recognize our self-transcendence toward God.

I do not want to suggest that the *content* of what is sung is immaterial. The intellectual content of church hymns, for example, ought to be a matter of grave concern, and I will treat this further below in a discussion of the relationship between beauty and ideology.

Feminist Views of Beauty

Feminist criticisms of religious traditions have largely focused on the structural and ideational barriers to women in those traditions. Feminists have examined the ways in which women have been kept from full participation in religious tradition. They have suggested social and structural changes in religious traditions or suggested that women abandon many religious traditions altogether as hopelessly and irreformably patriarchal. The focus has been mainly on moral activity or its lack.

Alongside this focus on the need for change or reform in religious traditions, many feminists have had to grapple with what has seemed to them the inescapable pull toward those traditions. Elisabeth Schüssler Fiorenza, for instance, stays in the Christian church, saying, "My vision of Christian life-style, responsibility, and community brought me to reject the culturally imposed role of women and not vice versa. What was this liberating vision that came through to me despite all patriarchal packaging and sexist theological systematization?"[12] Still other feminists have rejected traditional religions and sought out new religious traditions. For those who have turned to feminist religious traditions, such as worship of the Goddess, the primary focus has usually not been on the truth claims made by such religious traditions but on the experiential or ritual aspects.

As I have read accounts of women seeking new feminist religious options, I am convinced that what I have been calling the aesthetic dimension is a primary concern. Symbolizing and ritualizing women's religious experience have been central to new religious options for women. Women have sought to express their religious tradition through song, poetry, dance, and the creation of artistic objects. Because traditional religions have not taken women's experiences seriously, many women have sought satisfaction of experience elsewhere.

The paradox described by Elisabeth Schüssler Fiorenza also has an aesthetic dimension. Despite the fact that many women have found religious traditions oppressive in terms of beliefs or ethical implications, they find themselves still drawn into and involved in those same traditions. In part, of course, women remain in patriarchal traditions because they think that patriarchy is not the last word to be said in the tradition, because rethinking and reform of belief and conduct seem possible and necessary. But we ought not downplay the role of the aesthetic in decisions to remain. If, despite its overt and covert patriarchy, the drama of the Mass still moves one, it does so, in part at least, because it evokes in one a felt response as well as an intellectual and moral one. This does not mean that one can easily isolate the various responses, or say that only the level of feeling or experience matters, or that the level of feeling itself should remain unanalyzed. Feminists know only too well that when the beauty of the immediate experience passes they will be left with a religious organization that neither views them or treats them as full human beings. Feminists also know from other venues that feeling can be manipulated so as to be used for oppressive ends. Truth, goodness, and beauty are intimately related and, although they may be distinguished, cannot be separated as we try to live out our lives.

Feminists often speak of the importance of taking women's experiences into account. That has meant most centrally women's concrete and particular experiences of a variety of types of oppression. Feminists, in particular Rosemary Radford

Ruether, have also taken a major part in pointing out the destructive and oppressive nature of dualisms that subordinate body to mind and spirit, women to men, and nonhuman creatures to human ones.[13] One of the important goals of most forms of feminism has been to create possibilities for holistic, integrated existence for women, existence that recognizes women's interconnection with one another and with the whole of the universe. Although the possibility of holistic existence certainly has a crucial political or moral dimension, it also has an aesthetic dimension. Women should be enabled to enjoy their lives to the fullest. Women seek beauty.

"Beauty" is a term that has certainly had negative consequences for women in a number of ways. Instead of fostering beauty as a part of self-creation, ideals of beauty have been foisted on women. Women have often been seen as artifacts, objects of art, created by another or for another rather than themselves. Women have been forced by social pressures to measure up to certain "standards" of beauty, those standards being defined by others. The current "ideal" of female beauty is one that only a very small percentage of the female population could ever attain, and, therefore, its ideological uses to reinforce the oppression of women are enormous. If, as a woman, you do not "measure up" (and who does?) you are somehow not valuable as a woman. Note that *value* here is used ideologically by a dominant group to protect its own interests as arbiters of value.

I am using the term *beauty* to describe aesthetic value, the value of enjoyment or satisfaction of experience because of its long use in the history of thought. I mean the term to be understood broadly rather than narrowly, and I do have hopes that it can be reclaimed and used for nonideological purposes. That said, I do not think that the term *beauty* is the only possible way to name what is at issue here.

Audre Lorde uses the term *eros* to talk about many of the same facets of human life that I treat under the categories of "beauty," "worthy of enjoyment," or "satisfaction of experience." For Lorde, *erotic* designates an internal sense of "satisfaction" or "completion." It is "not a question only of what we do; it is a question of how acutely and fully we can feel in the doing."[14] The erotic is relational; it connects us to others in the world. It can arise in response to music and works of art.

The erotic is minimized and distorted by being equated with pornography or obscenity:

> There is one reason why the erotic is so feared, and so often relegated to the bedroom alone, when it is recognized at all. For once we begin to feel deeply in all the aspects of our lives, we begin to demand from ourselves and from our life-pursuits that they feel in accordance with that joy which we know ourselves to be capable of. Our erotic knowledge empowers us, becomes a lens through which we scrutinize all aspects of our existence, forcing us to evaluate those aspects honestly in terms of their relative meaning within our lives. And this is a grave responsibility, projected from within each of us, not to settle for the convenient, the shoddy, the conventionally expected, nor the merely safe.[15]

For Lorde, the source and ground of the erotic is internal to individuals, for she worries about the imposition of external rules and directives. Although I would argue that beauty or the erotic is grounded in the whole of reality and finds its source in God, I am not portraying a God who issues alien directives to command obedience, but one who offers the possibility of the creation of the very values Lorde lauds. Lorde looks for what she calls the erotic only among "women-identified women" and recognizes how it has been distorted by an "exclusively european-american male tradition."[16] Although Lorde is correct to see the possibility of distortion, the erotic value she describes could be shared by women and men in a society that valued the connections of which she speaks.

To define the search for beauty as the search for a balance of harmony and intensity fosters the wholeness and interconnection that feminists seek. For example, Marilyn French defines feminist art, asserting that "feminist art suggests that things are connected as well as divided, that a person is not always at war with herself or her world, that in fact people seek to live harmoniously with themselves and their world *even though they can't control either.*"[17] Such a definition of beauty recognizes the value of each individual part of the universe and its ability to contribute to the beauty of the whole. Beauty is not anthropocentric. This view sees beauty as a value not just for the perceiver of some beautiful object, but also as a value for the one who fosters or creates beauty. In this sense, beauty is a relational value and not a static quality or set of qualities.

To see beauty as a balance of harmony and intensity also recognizes that there are many varied ways to create and appreciate beauty. Individual and communal taste (also, as I will later argue, combined with judgments about truth and goodness) plays a large role in the way beauty is perceived. Beauty is beauty in context. This allows feminists the possibility of judging what is said to be beautiful not only in and of itself but also in relation to its total context. Beauty, like justice, needs to take the whole into account. If what is called beauty creates a balance of harmony and intensity that only a certain group can appreciate or in which only a small portion of the world's existents can participate, then beauty has been turned into ideology. French articulates a similar sentiment specifically in relation to art:

> Art nourishes a society, feeds it; sturdy not delicate, it arises from the life of a people like food from the ground, teaching us what we do not know, reminding us of what we tend to forget, emphasizing what is important, grieving over pain, celebrating vitality. It is useful and beautiful and moral—not moralistic. The standards I hold for feminist art are thus, as you have probably guessed, my standards in life. And that is what I believe an art, any art, ought to be: an expression of a vision that is at once a belief and a faith—belief in humanity and faith in its future. I have always accepted the Horatian definition of the purpose of art—to teach and to delight—and I believe feminist art can make us better, just as I think a feminist world would make us better. But art is not just a moral act. There is a last principle which is not feminist but truly universal: vitality. Art must create the illusion of "felt life," as Henry James suggested.[18]

Beauty across Religious Traditions

If I am present to the worship or ritual life of a religious community other than my own, I might well be drawn into the experience aesthetically, even if I am not exactly sure on a cognitive level what is happening. The ambiance of the place, its decoration and artwork, the symbols used, the way in which words are employed (even if I do not understand the language), my perceptions of the involvement of participants—all these might well address me and draw me in. I might find the experience beautiful or satisfying in terms of finding it a balance of harmony and intensity. I might begin to understand how it feels to be part of this community even if I am not fully conscious of the community's cognitive and moral dimensions. I might begin to experience what it is that the community values through its concretization of religious experience in ritual and artifact.

The aesthetic experience that one has of a religious tradition not one's own can draw one into further analysis and exploration of the tradition. Aesthetic appreciation can lead to exchange, comparison aimed at drawing out similarities and differences, and dialogue. It can lead to questions of how the experience is informed by views of what is true and good. To recognize the aesthetic dimension of religious tradition is to see how religion grasps and involves whole human beings, not just disembodied minds or spirits. To see the importance of the felt quality of religious experience points us toward seeing religious traditions as ways of life, as ways of teaching us to be human, to be self-creative and creative of value for others. The aesthetic dimension is yet another *entrée* into the religious lives of others. If the argument of this book has been correct, to recognize the multidimensionality of one's own religious life and the religious lives of others gives access to one another's lives in many meaningful ways.[19]

If cognitive interpretations of religious symbols are the point at which adherents of religious traditions part company, perhaps there can be a measure of shared aesthetic experience in the face of a great work of religious art that can then foster one's understanding of another. It is also possible, I am certain, to have one's cognitive understandings broadened or called into question by aesthetic experience, by the experience of another's creation of beauty that points beyond itself as beautiful first to an intuition, then to an understanding of the vision of reality that underlies the experience of beauty. When I enter the Buddhist Wat Traimit Withayaram Worawitarn in Bangkok and encounter the twelve-foot high, solid gold statue of the Buddha, I am first amazed by the sight. The huge statue gleams in the dim light. Then I notice the care of craft, the proportion, the delicacy of the detail. The statue also has a context. It is surrounded by gifts of fruit and flowers, by lighted candles, by worshipers who do not regard it first as an objet d'art but as a religious symbol. Through the combination of great beauty and particular context and content of the statue, I am drawn into the experience of the worshipers. At the Kyongbokkung Palace in Seoul I encounter a perfectly square pond with a perfectly round island in its exact center. It is an exquisite sight, perfectly balanced and beautifully maintained. I am led through its Taoist symbolism to reflect on the nature and balance of reality as whole.

Beauty can transform one who experiences it. One's way of seeing the world can be challenged by an aesthetic presentation of a world that differs from one's own. It calls one up short to experience in a religious context a balance of harmony and intensity that comes to one as new and unexpected. A mandala, for instance, with its intricate design focused on a center point, might well force one to reflect on one's own linear view of the world and its interrelationships.

Beauty Includes Truth and Goodness

Truth, goodness, and beauty are intimately related to one another. Indeed, Charles Hartshorne argues that beauty is the inclusive category, of which truth and goodness are forms:

> Values may be considered under three heads: acting rightly, thinking correctly, and experiencing well or satisfyingly. In other words, goodness, truth and (in a generalized sense) beauty. But, as Peirce held, the order is wrong. The basic value is the intrinsic value of experiencing, as a unity of feeling inclusive of whatever volition and thought the experience contains, and exhibiting harmony or beauty. If we know what experience is, at its best or most beautiful, then and only then can we know how it is right to act; for the value of action is in what it contributes to experiences. Thinking, Peirce held, is one form of acting, and hence logic as a normative science is a branch of ethics. Both presuppose aesthetics, in a generalized sense: the study of what makes experiences good in themselves.[20]

Hartshorne's position makes good feminist sense. Feminists have argued that experience is primary, and that too little attention has been paid to experience in general and in particular to experiences of over half the population. Although they have not usually articulated it in aesthetic terms, feminists have understood that women have been robbed of fullness of existence or the satisfaction of experience in a large number of ways.

Hartshorne's position also makes good feminist sense in recognizing the individual's need for integrity as well as interconnections among human beings and among all creatures in the universe. Beauty is a value to which all parts of the universe can contribute. Truth and goodness are values to which only reflective beings can contribute. Beauty is a value which takes the whole of an individual into account rather than fragmenting her or him into mind or spirit and body. The inclusive value of beauty is the value that integrates rather than separates, provides well-rounded rather than one-dimensional experience.

In our lives, although one might well distinguish beauty from truth and goodness, if one separates them one does so at the peril of not recognizing the effect of their interconnection for existence in the universe. For example, the current Western standards of female beauty cannot be separated from the effects of this standard on the overall values that are assigned to women, which values, in turn, have an effect on the way women are treated politically and socially. If women's prime role is to be aesthetically pleasing for men, this grants women only instrumental value, not value in and for themselves.

Beauty influences goodness and vice versa. Standards of morality help to determine when beauty is being ideologized in the service of one particular group rather than another. Nothing exists in isolation. One might be inspired by beauty, by what prompts enjoyment, to live one's life in a particular way. Insofar as beauty informs action in the world it can also be called into question by standards governing moral activity. The search for beauty for oneself or one's group may run roughshod over the possibilities of both goodness and beauty for another. What purports to be beauty may in fact be destructive to individuals or corporate bodies. If creation of what is considered "beauty" involves, for example, the forced labor of human beings who are not themselves allowed to find satisfaction in that creation, beauty is compromised. The search for personal fulfillments of experience that, in moderation or in their proper relational contexts, might be both moral and aesthetic goods (I think here particularly of the aesthetic dimensions of food or sex) can also be distorted and thus harmful to other individuals or to a broader community. We need to keep reminding ourselves that beauty is a process of interaction rather than a set of qualities possessed by something or other. We also need to keep reminding ourselves that the discernment of beauty cannot be separated from the discernment of goodness:

Morality necessarily depends in part on aesthetic discernment, on taste: taste as apperception, enabling us to recognize moral implications in aesthetic forms; as appraisal, enabling us to estimate the morally good (or bad) within the beautiful (or ugly); and as appreciation, enabling us personally to value the aesthetically manifest good or to reject the bad, and hence to be disposed to act.[21]

Truth is expressed in various ways. At its most precise, allowing the least possible room for misunderstanding, truth is expressed in literal language. And there is an aesthetic component to literal language that glories in the beauty of a finely crafted argument. But the finely crafted argument is also mostly one-dimensional. It does not, for most people, in and of itself speak to the whole human being, evoke the holistic response that is the satisfaction of experience, experience at its most fulfilling. Frank Burch Brown notes that religious traditions are not merely mediated through good argument, but also through symbol, liturgy, story, art:

> Even supposing that some of the truth in which Christianity has a stake can be arrived at directly by means of logic and metaphysics, it remains the case that, if any conceptualization is to be theologically convincing, it somehow must resonate with more primary religious or quasi-religious language and experience. And this frequently bears conspicuous aesthetic marks, as is evident in parable, apocalypse, liturgy, sacred song, spiritual exercises, the rhythms of ecclesial life, and even in the tensions and resolutions of moral and human relationships.[22]

Beauty may be used negatively in the service of one group or other; but it can also be a force for transformation. The experience of harmony and intensity can challenge us to see the world in new ways, to look at ourselves and our lives differently. Aesthetic experience gives rise to reflection not only on the experience of beauty, but on life as a whole, and thus one's life may be transformed. In turn, reflection colors the way beauty is seen and provides the context and categories for our experience of beauty.

The argument of this chapter is that beauty, like truth and goodness, indeed as inclusive of truth and goodness, is, in its various manifestations, the creative (often self-creative) response to basic experience of value, integrity, and interconnection. Judgments as to beauty are not just matters of personal taste. Unless what purports to be beauty expresses the value, integrity, and interconnection of primary experience, it is not beauty. Insofar as the categories of truth and goodness are subsets of the category beauty, they are appropriate ways to reflect on and judge the beautiful. For example, unless aesthetic discernment takes moral discernment into account, it will not be credible to those who are oppressed by the purportedly beautiful. Aesthetic discernment also needs to take into account the view of reality that is presented, recognizing that aesthetic forms will not be credible to those who do not share the presented view of reality. But, as we have seen, truth and goodness alone do not encompass the whole category. I suggested above, following Hartshorne, that beauty ought, finally, to be judged on whether it fosters a balance of harmony and intensity. Several matters require further comment, however.

First, there is much beauty to be created and enjoyed by existents in the universe (including, in the theistic view presented here, by God). But, given that some choices made by free creatures automatically exclude other choices, only a limited number of possible beauties is ever realized. Thus, the beauties of the universe are products of the free choices of creatures and God and can never be anticipated fully. It is pointless to compare the beauty of Beethoven's Fifth Symphony with the beauty of an Eleventh Symphony by Beethoven that *might* have been written.

Second, not only do I exclude some of my own choices by making others, my choices may exclude certain choices of others or may come into conflict with these choices. For beauty as well as for goodness, the question of scope is crucial to reflective judgment. Whom will this supposed beauty benefit? Whom will it harm? Free creatures will inevitably clash with other free creatures, both over the creation of moral goods and over the creation of aesthetic beauty. As in the question of moral good, judgment or discernment involves recognition of the scope of value as a whole as well as the possibility of any one individual creating value. There is no formulaic way to solve the problem of what gets precedence when values clash. In the case of reflective creatures who can anticipate outcomes and weigh the possible balances, however, discerning a maximal balance between harmony and intensity that is not just individual but broad in scope ought to be seen as a weighty responsibility. Harmony and intensity also apply to moral good. In the search for truth, goodness, and beauty, there is no pure altruism nor mere self-interest, only a myriad of ways of balancing the proportions of the two.[23] The decision is always how the two will be balanced as a self-creative individual makes choices.

Third, the balances of harmony and intensity that satisfy the enjoyment of experiencing individuals vary from species to species and from individual to individual. In addition, our social and cultural contexts influence our expectations and experiences of harmony and intensity. Thus, there is still a very large part to be played in aesthetic discernment by communal and individual taste or preferences.

Analyze it as I might, there are elements of appreciation in aesthetic experience that are, finally, communal and personal. As a Westerner I have learned to hear music through the structure of the eight-tone scale. I do not know of any way to judge that this is aesthetically "better" or "worse" than a pentatonic scale. Yet my appreciation of music is colored by this context. This does not mean that I cannot respond positively to music based on other patterns of construction or that such music cannot be experientially satisfying for me. Indeed, such music represents a challenge to my way of hearing music and thus to my views of the balance of harmony and intensity. Yet I hear the music in my context; and even when I am conscious of the various factors involved in my hearing it as I do, I am still left to make personal judgments about its place, value, worth in my life.

Likewise, the class-consciousness in which I was raised points me toward valuing classical music over country and western music. As a child of the 1960s, I learned to love folk music and rock n' roll. Although I can point to the lack of complexity of *some* country and western music, to the insipidity of some of its lyrics, and so on, one could find equally insipid classical music and rock n' roll. My context affects the way I hear the music and, finally, my preferences in music are my own, shared with other members of my sociocultural group. My recognition of how my preference is in part influenced by my social class should give me pause, however, to look again at these preferences and to see where these preferences might impinge on the way I see and treat others as individuals and groups.

The aesthetic dimension of life is informed widely by one's total contact with the world. Even things whose primary function might be to evoke enjoyment are tied to the totality of life, not just to a separable aesthetic faculty. The aesthetically enjoyable comes in many ways.

Religious traditions express in symbol, in story, in liturgy, in prayer and ritual, in song and dance, and in a host of other ways a view of the world and the consequences that should follow from that. Insofar as the presentation of any given religion's worldview and ethos grasps us and draws us in to its purview, we have experienced its aesthetic power. Insofar as we respond by trying to replicate the experience we ourselves have had, we seek to re-create that aesthetic experience for others.

This book has argued that the ground of our religious life as human beings is an experience of value, integrity, and inter- connection. It has argued that the various ways of being religious are responses to primary experience embodied and expressed in concrete and historical forms. Insofar as we experience a religious tradition as addressed to ourselves as whole human beings rather than as fragmented into discrete parts, we have been grasped by its aesthetic dimension. The aesthetic is not just an appeal to emotion, if emotion is seen as a realm of the human being separable from the totality of what it means to be human, separable from rational or critical functioning, or separable from the will to act.

The aesthetic dimension of religious experience invites the engagement of the whole human being in the experience of being religious in a particular way. It is possible to appeal only to emotion, without regard for the implications of that appeal for truth or goodness. Sentimental appeals can be designed to elicit quick emotional response without any depth dimension. But this is to disregard the grounding of aesthetic experience in a particular worldview. It is also, usually, to ignore the balance between harmony and intensity that is productive of fullness of experience in favor of quickened intensity that does not last.

The aesthetic dimension of religious experience gives depth to our experience of being drawn to a particular tradition. The multitude of forms in which religious traditions can be and are expressed points to the complexity of human life and fullness of human existence. It points to the need for intensity as well as harmony, and for a variety of entry points into the religious tradition. When we experience ultimate reality, however it is conceived and symbolized, as having relevance *for us* as whole human beings, to the fullness and satisfaction of our lives as a whole, and to the rest of the creatures with whom we share the universe, the experience has a dimension of beauty.

In a theistic rendering of the experience of value, integrity, and interconnection, God ought not to be equated with beauty. Yet our experience of God as of value and being valued includes experience of beauty. God is more than beauty, yet beauty as the ultimate value is an aspect of God. When, in response to God's valuing of us, we seek to create value, we create beauty. Those, in turn, who experience the beauty we create can be drawn by that to the matrix, the underlying source of the possibility of all beauty. When the beauty we create is somehow, in form or content or function, explicitly associated with the God in response to whom it arises, the cognitive and the aesthetic can interact to focus and articulate our experience as experience of God.

Religious traditions that are not theistic point in the association of aesthetic and cognitive dimensions to different construals of ultimate reality. As one is grasped by the aesthetic dimension of another's tradition, the cognitive dimension itself may come under challenge. One must always ask if one's experience supports the interpretation it is being given.

It is the aesthetic dimension of religion more than any other that points to the fullness of human existence, indeed of existence as a whole. Here beauty, goodness, and truth have been presented not as three parallel categories, but as nesting dolls, as it were, beauty being inclusive of goodness, which is, in its turn, inclusive of truth. Religious traditions present not just ways of thinking or acting, but total ways of being human. They are adequate ways of being human insofar as they provide for the possibility of the fullness of existence, understood here to include not only human existence but existence in the universe. Fullness of existence is understood to include the creation of value for others, the creation of the possibility of others creating values to their fullest potential, and expression of the grounding of those values in some conception of reality.

In this book we began with the specificity of the Christian tradition and argued from it to the more general claims it seemed to be making about what we have here called truth, goodness, and beauty. We also began with the argument that religious traditions were often ideologized in particular ways to benefit particular groups. Specifically, I argued that feminist analysis was crucial to the de-ideologizing of Christianity and other religious traditions. As we looked at the more generalized claims concerning truth, goodness, and beauty we began to look at how these general claims might function in interreligious discussions. In the final chapter, we will pull together the strands provided here into the outlines of a feminist Christian theology for a religiously plural age.

7
Contours of a
Feminist Christian Theology
for a Religiously Plural Age

This chapter will seek to draw together the strands of the book's arguments to outline a feminist Christian theology for a religiously plural age. It will seek to show how recognition that christology makes claims about truth, goodness, and beauty opens up possibilities for interreligious understanding and fosters feminist goals. I begin by returning to the situations posed at the end of the first chapter.

• In chapter 1 I raised issues of how and why a committee trying to settle on a topic and format for Jewish-Christian dialogue settled on issues of poverty rather than issues of women in our respective traditions and society. The Jewish-Christian dialogue on issues of poverty did, in fact, take place. We brought together panels of people over several evenings and had quite productive discussions on issues important to all of us. Although a wide range of views was expressed, the differences did not emerge along religious lines but along other lines of social analysis. Those inclined to a more "socialist" or communitarian point of view saw poverty and its causes and solutions in one way. Those inclined to a more individualist or classical liberal point of view saw the issues another way. There was a broad spectrum of views in between. Jews and Christians found themselves together along the spectrum. Clearly, one thing such a dialogue did was to show that, although there is a connection between one's faith and one's commitments to action in the world, there was no one "Christian" or "Jewish" way to act. Because at each point on the spectrum of analysis and action there were both Christians and Jews, any notion that one or the other tradition was morally superior was quickly dispelled. We could agree on strategies for change across religious lines.

That we chose a topic designed to elicit discussion on goodness rather than on the particular symbols of our respective traditions or on matters of truth or beauty revealed a lot about our instincts about where commonality could fairly easily be found. It also revealed a profound worry on the part of those who were not scholars or experts that unless one was an "expert" one ought not to discuss matters of religious symbols or truth claims. When we toyed with the possibility of a discussion of liturgy or prayer, the group seemed to consider such things partly ineffable and partly a matter of taste or choice and therefore not a proper topic of discussion. The group clearly was more comfortable with making and discussing moral choices. For the most part, the eventual discussions stopped short of the religious motivations for the moral choices we made.

The fact that we did not discuss women was, however, significant. It showed that many were uncomfortable enough with the subject that they were not willing to expose themselves or their religious tradition to the scrutiny of others. Women are equal to men in both our traditions, some said, let us not get hung up on the question of leadership or participation. Women have their specific roles and men have theirs. They are separate but equal. For some, the topic of women was simply not important enough to devote time and energy to discussion.

• At present in the Canadian province where I live, in the "public" school system one can begin the day with a reading from one of the world's religious traditions, but one cannot begin with prayer. One can teach about religion, but one cannot impose one particular tradition as superior or indoctrinate others into a particular tradition. Because the system began as a "Protestant" school system, many people bemoan the loss of "Christian" values and the loss of the celebration of Christian holidays.

The Ontario government policy, which does, for reasons of historical legislation and tradition, also allow for full government funding for Roman Catholic schools, has been challenged by other religious groups to provide a government-funded

Jewish school system, Muslim school system, and so on. Such court challenges have to date been unsuccessful because the courts have ruled that no one is denied education on the basis of religion, and therefore the government is not obligated to fund a host of religious school systems.

The government policy on religious education in public schools recognizes the religious diversity of the province. It also recognizes religion as something that can be taught about and understood. One does not have to belong to a religious tradition to know about it. Some of those who disagree with the current government policy find no way to distinguish the specific symbols of the Christian tradition from the more general claims that this book has argued are embodied in those specific symbols. They argue that there are values and truths uniquely "Christian" and that such values are superior to all others.

According to the argument of this book, Christian symbols, like all other religious symbols, embody more general claims about reality. This does not mean that one should only study or talk about the general claims, leaving the symbols to the religious. It does mean, however, that one ought not to study the symbols in isolation from the claims about reality and the way of life they are seen to imply. Those who lament the loss of "Christian" values often do not know that many similar values are embodied elsewhere.

I quit going to Sunday School when I was twelve because I felt I was being cheated out of an education in favor of indoctrination. I asked my teacher how I could know that Christianity was the religion I ought to choose as my own when I did not know about any other religious traditions. She responded that we did not have time to study any other religions, since it was so crucial to learn about Christianity. She was, I think, fearful of her own ignorance about other traditions and fearful that she would not be able to defend Christianity in the face of questions about it.

Many who are cultural Christians want their children to learn "Christianity" in school so they too will be culturally Christian. But such cultural Christianity is not usually a questing for answers to deeply felt questions so much as it is an insurance policy against the unknown. Unfortunately, many churches foster the same attitude to questioning, implying that only nonbelievers raise questions. In the context of the church, however, the kind of questioning that leads to reflection on the claims about truth, goodness, and beauty embodied in Christian tradition is often discouraged in favor of a fideistic acceptance of authority. Reflective faith, response to grace, and commitment in one's whole being can be replaced by living on the basis of someone else's authority. Lack of reflective faith can lead both to the refusal to see the shortcomings of one's own articulation and living out of one's own religious tradition (in this case, Christianity) and to a refusal to draw lines of similarity and comparison between one's own religious tradition and that of others.

• The students from my "Women and Religion" class, although they have profound reservations about the religious choices made by a fairly traditional Muslim woman who visits the class to talk about her life as a woman and a Muslim, have great difficulty figuring out how to deal with these reservations. They want to be respectful of her and of her choices. They acknowledge cultural as well as religious differences (even though my visitor is Canadian, she did not grow up in Canada). They have many fewer reservations about criticizing and judging the religious choices of the Christian women who come to visit (usually among them a Roman Catholic nun). Their questions for the Jewish women who come are more critical than those for the Christian women, but less than those for the traditional Muslim woman.

Their reactions are, in part, an outgrowth of recognition of their own cultural imperialism and their society's Christian imperialism. Most of the women are from backgrounds that could be described as "secularized Christian," that is, they do not attend religious services, and perhaps never have, but they might look to the church for services at times of crisis. Some of the students are active in Christian churches. Occasionally there is a Jewish or Muslim student.

On the one hand, their reactions to the Jewish and Muslim visitors seek to respect the context from which the visitors come. They recognize the importance of cultural and religious diversity and the place of personal choice among the various options available. They do not want to impose their own assumptions on the visitors. On the other hand, they are often profoundly uncomfortable with the choices made by these visitors and are trying to figure out whether such discomfort is legitimate. They are casting about for some more broadly based criteria through which to understand both the visitor's choices and their own reactions. The categories of truth, goodness, and beauty suggested here provide some evaluative criteria for approaching a variety of religious options, thus giving the students more than the "take the whole or leave it all" approach that they incline to at first thought. Such a nuanced approach also allows for the possibility of both understanding and evaluating another's choices in a multifaceted way, rather than as an undifferentiated whole.

• In the last several years the United Church of Canada has been attempting to formulate a theological understanding of its relationship to other religious traditions. Like many other Christian denominations, the United Church has had to face up to the fact that it exists in a pluralistic world, and that much rethinking must in consequence be done. The denomination is diverse, and there is no agreed-on position vis-à-vis other traditions. The denomination includes those who wish to continue the traditional Christian view that Jesus is the sole and sufficient savior for the whole world. But it also includes those who think that we need to draw what is useful from a variety of religious traditions, and that no one religious tradition should hold a privileged place. The 1990 General Council (the national church governing body), in response to many petitions asking it to affirm "the unique saving significance of Jesus Christ," passed a resolution affirming "Jesus Christ as the cornerstone of the Church" and affirming the church's "intent to continue to be faithful to the historic and living truth of the Christian faith."[1] In 1993, an earlier report from the Interchurch-Interfaith Committee on "Towards a Renewed Understanding of Ecumenism" was returned to the committee for reworking, largely because many at the General Council felt it was missing a strong affirmation of Jesus Christ as savior.[2] The major tension lies in trying to affirm Christian identity and continuing commitment to the Christian church alongside recognition that traditional Christian claims to be the only true religion, to be morally superior to other traditions, are seriously challenged in today's world.

In many ways, the discussions of religious pluralism in the United Church have been carried on as if the only two options were (1) versions of the exclusivist and inclusivist arguments that salvation is offered only or primarily and most fully in Jesus Christ, or (2) a version of the pluralist argument that to claim salvation in Jesus Christ automatically excludes and demeans all other religious options, and thus, that we should give up all claims to find salvation in Jesus Christ or should a priori assume that all religious ways are equally valid ways of salvation.

The approach offered in this book is, I think, helpful for the dilemma faced by the Interchurch-Interfaith Committee as it seeks to rewrite its report. The argument of this book is that one can claim Christian identity and understand the Christian witness of faith to be making generally defensible claims that it is worthy of belief, that it fosters activity worthy of being done, and that overall it provides that which is worthy of enjoyment, while not dismissing the possibility that other religious traditions could do the same. Such an argument, which begins with an understanding of Jesus Christ as representative rather than constitutive of salvation and continues to explore the claims christology makes in terms of truth, goodness, and beauty, provides an alternative to the dilemma being played out in this church and, I suspect, in many others. It provides a way to understand commitment to a religious tradition as to a way of life that embodies an adequate and accurate view of reality and enjoins one to morally responsible and enjoyable activity without asserting that there is only one set of religious symbols in which justifiable claims to truth, goodness, and beauty could be adequately embodied.

• The protests against clearcutting old growth forest in Clayoquot Sound, British Columbia, arise, undoubtedly, from a variety of motivations. But all are based in the notion that destruction for human gain of one of the few remaining unexploited portions of the world is morally wrong. The protests have taken many forms, including physically blocking the logging roads, organizing information distribution on various roads near the logging sites and in front of the British Columbia legislative buildings, and letter writing. Some, perhaps many, of the protesters would articulate a religious motivation underlying the particular action of protesting the logging activity. Yet the particular religious symbol systems to which appeal is made vary widely. On one particular day of the protests the Victoria paper carried a front-page picture and story of the arrests of Starhawk and an Anglican priest.[3] Although these two, I would venture to guess, would articulate the particular and specific religious motivations for their protest activity quite differently, the resulting activity was the same. This example leads me to think that the notion that general claims about goodness and beauty are implied in the more specific and symbolic claims of Christianity (and other religious traditions) is essential to a conversation that might take place between Starhawk and the priest about the movement from religious conviction to particular activity.

• I stare at Marc Chagall's painting, *The Praying Jew,* and I am drawn into its ambiance. There is depth and texture in the picture as a whole. The tradition is represented in prayer shawl and phylacteries. There is wisdom in the elderly face, and the eyes of the praying man are not focused on me. They look upward. The background is, in places, almost translucent. The painting speaks to me of human suffering, and of the possibility of transcendence. To me, the praying Jew represents the long history and heritage of Judaism. It evokes a different sense of history and connection than I often experience in the presence of works of art that are overtly Christian in subject matter. I "enjoy" the painting. It adds depth and richness to my own life. In its color, its texture, its composition, its subject matter, it is complex. It invites response, questions. It enriches my life with a satisfying balance of harmony and intensity.

Yet the painting in other ways excludes me. As a non-Jew, as a woman, I am not invited to participate fully in that of which it reminds me and to which it calls me. While as a whole the experience grasps me and draws me into its spell, its subject matter both includes and excludes me.

Sustaining Christian Identity

Can the claims of Christianity be sustained in the face of serious questions arising from feminism and religious pluralism? This book has argued that, although they have often been used patriarchally and imperialistically, Christian claims about Jesus as the Christ are not, of necessity, either patriarchal or imperialistic.

Claims about Jesus as the Christ need to be justified in light of their own sources and in light of contemporary questions but, if the argument of this book has been valid, they do not need to be abandoned in favor of other religious claims that would present fewer problems for feminists or for those sensitive to the realities of various religious traditions.

There is no generic religiosity. One is always religious in a particular way. One employs a particular set of symbols, and finds oneself as part of a particular religious history. The particularity and historicity of our lives need to be taken seriously in religious traditions as elsewhere. I have argued that Christians do make general claims in their religious tradition, but that they make these general claims through the particular and the specific.

A major point of the book has been that one can argue for the claims that Christians make for and about their symbol system and tradition in a way that, although it might not find acceptance in all quarters, the arguments are more generally accessible. The book began with the particularity of Christian claims about Jesus. When those claims were examined, it became clear that one does not necessarily need to see Jesus Christ as constitutive of salvation. Indeed, to see Jesus as constituting salvation, as the only contact with or conduit of God's grace, leaves unaccounted for a host of points important to Christian tradition. Jesus as the Christ does not constitute salvation or contact with God's love or grace. Rather, he re-presents or embodies God's grace or revelation, and thus in him God offers a salvation that is universal and universally accessible.

Christology answers a human question about fullness of existence. In making claims about Jesus, christology makes more general claims about the structure of reality and how we should live in response. The Christian tradition sees God as the source of fullness of life and points toward human response to God in a way that fosters such fullness. In the Christian tradition God is the source and ground of life. Life in response to God means a life that fosters the possibility of fullness of existence for all with whom we share the world.

When we look at the more general claims implied by specific assertions about Jesus, we see that they can take and have taken many forms in the history of Christianity. Not all views of God are equivalent. Not all demands for action on behalf of the neighbor bring about the same results. Not all experience is equally satisfying. Thus, as one looks at the more general claims made through the Christian symbols, one needs to look not only at their provenance in biblical witness but also at the ways in which such claims could be justified by arguments credible to those who do not align themselves with those symbols. The Christian witness of faith, it is argued here, presents a view of reality (including God as its ground and focus) that can be claimed as true. This witness of faith evokes responses to reality that foster fullness of existence by eliciting and sanctioning goodness and beauty. Truth, goodness, and beauty are neither unique to nor defined by the Christian tradition. Even though the claim is made here that truth, goodness, and beauty are re-presented in and evoked by the Christian tradition, or, more accurately, in and by certain understandings of the Christian tradition, no claim is made that the Christian tradition is the only religious tradition adequately or accurately to re-present or evoke truth, goodness, and beauty. Other religious traditions would also need to be presented in terms of their own particular and general claims before any such judgments could be made. As Hugo Meynell puts it:

138

> What has to be aimed at is a careful articulation of the content and implications of one's own and rival sets of beliefs, so as to determine just what real mutual contradictions there are, if any, when the differences in language, culture, and general background of those maintaining the sets of beliefs are fully taken into account.[4]

Christians claim that the ultimate reality to whom we relate is God. In terms of making a consistent and coherent argument that the universe is most adequately understood as theistic and in terms of answering questions raised by feminism and by the plurality of religious traditions, not all views of God are the same. This book has argued that panentheism provides the most adequate concept of God. Clearly, to put forth such a view of ultimate reality as panentheistic does not answer all the questions that arise for those who do not so conceive the world.

In terms of interreligious understanding, what I have sought to do here is to set out the reasons that could be adduced for seeing ultimate reality as God and to set out what conception of God such reasons might support. The result is, I hope, a more nuanced view of reality than simply theistic versus nontheistic. One can then enter into discussion of this view of reality in several ways. One can examine the arguments for primary experience that I have claimed points to God as its genesis. One can debate whether theism best accounts for primary experience. One can ask whether other accountings of primary experience might be as adequate or more so. One can ask whether to name ultimate reality "God" is automatically to import to this reality concepts that I have explicitly rejected here.

In terms of feminist questions, the naming of ultimate reality is crucial. Feminists rightly recognize that our naming of ultimate reality has consequences for both thought and activity. To name God as solely and only male is harmful to women. Feminists also recognize the harm in seeing God as a controlling and manipulative deity who contravenes human freedoms and creativity.

The theism argued for in this book does not portray God as male or as controlling and manipulative. It does not argue that God is only properly recognized and understood from within the Christian tradition. God is related to all that exists and responsive to all that exists. God wills and fosters the fullness of existence that, I have argued, is implied in Christian claims. But I have not by any means argued that fullness of existence could not be symbolized by other traditions in other ways or fostered by other traditions.

Finally, however, the Christian tradition is theistic. It does name ultimate reality as God or deity. Thus, it cannot simply accommodate all other ways of seeing reality. It may well be able to accommodate *some* other ways of seeing reality. As others set forth alternate views of reality, Christians must examine and consider them and the arguments adduced for them. In the final analysis, judgments must be made.

In the Christian tradition, human beings are called to love their neighbors. As with views of God, views of love of neighbor have varied much in Christian history. The notion of "neighbor" has been more or less broadly defined. The sort of activity required has been seen at times as one-to-one action for another, disregarding the social circumstances that cause the situation at hand. Here the argument is that primary experience of integrity, interconnection, and value, together with the concrete and specific questions and claims of the oppressed, point toward a view of moral goodness that is universal in scope. It leaves none out of account as claimants to human activity to create the conditions for fullness of existence, and it includes not only individual action but our actions in structuring and living through our political and social relationships. The specific context provides the concrete data necessary for determining what particular moral activities are warranted in any given instance.

In a religiously plural situation, it may first of all be possible to agree on specific courses of action across religious lines before one enters into discussion about the sources or motivations for those actions. This is in large part because of shared social and political contexts that provide areas of mutual concern and of mutual possibility for action. Also, even if religious traditions name ultimate reality in a variety of ways, most religious traditions posit ultimate reality beyond the solitary individual or small community, broadening the scope of concern from the beginning. To explicate love of neighbor in terms of a search for wholeness and integrity and a recognition of the interconnection of all that exists provides a general claim to which other traditions might well relate in their reflections on Christianity.

The search for integrity and wholeness and the recognition of interconnection are goals that most feminists could espouse and upon which feminists can begin concretely to build more equitable social and political structures. One could well come to these goals from a variety of directions. And one could embody or enact them in a variety of ways. Feminist consciousness acts as a corrective to the narrowing of the scope of claimants to moral good. Feminist criticism serves as one important pointer to the gap between religious ideals and activity. It also provides a constant reminder that general principles for activity are meaningless unless they are enacted.

The Christian tradition speaks to the whole human being, not only evoking a response of moral goodness, but evoking and fostering fullness of life in all its dimensions. Human life seeks satisfaction beyond the mere fulfilling of bodily needs. In response to the Christian witness, many have enriched their own lives and the lives of others through the fostering of beauty or the satisfaction of experience in its many forms. The integrity, wholeness, and interconnection that can be fostered through human moral agency can also be fostered through creation of beauty. And humans are not the only creatures capable of creating beauty for others. Beauty points us beyond the notion of value as the sole province of human creatures.

The beauty of the objects and ceremonies of religious traditions can draw one into the experiences of worshipers in other traditions. They can give access to a depth of experience beyond the given explanations. Aesthetic value or beauty can, like goodness, be narrowed in scope so as to make what is called beauty into a mere instrumental value for someone else. Beauty, the fullest satisfaction of experience, integrating the interests of the individual part of the universe with the creation of value as value for the whole, is an ideal that most feminists would find attractive.

The Christian tradition is not an irreducible and incommensurable set of symbols and practices that have no relation to other forms of human life. In the specific language, symbols, and rituals of the Christian tradition are contained more general claims about the nature of reality and of how, given this reality, human beings ought to live. Christians have historically understood themselves to be making claims not just to be seeing the world in one particular way among others but to be seeing the world as it is.

This book has provided one way to look at the general implications of the claims that Christians make. If Christians are making claims that hold beyond the bounds of Christian believers, that is, if they take themselves to be affirming that which is, in general, worthy of belief, action, and enjoyment, then arguments need to be adduced to support these claims. One of the purposes of this book has been to ascertain what grounds might be given for Christian claims that the Christian tradition paints a true picture of reality and fosters moral and aesthetic value.

The project of critically reflecting on the Christian tradition, which is the project of all Christian theology, is here focused by two sets of questions arising with particular force from the present contexts in which Christianity finds itself: questions raised by feminist analysis and questions raised by the recognition of the plurality of world religious traditions. Christianity has often itself been patriarchal and has aligned itself with patriarchal forces in societies. Christianity has often asserted itself imperialistically as the best or only valid way to be religious. There is no doubt that in many of its lived-out forms Christianity is both patriarchal and imperialistic. As a theologian, my main concern was not with examining those lived-out forms in detail, as important as they are, but in asking about whether those lived-out forms bear an inherent relationship to the ideals of the Christian tradition. In other words, must Christianity be patriarchal and imperialistic? Is Christianity inherently patriarchal and imperialistic?

Giving a negative answer to these questions does not downplay the difficult work of embodying in Christian life the alternative view of Christian claims put forward here. What I have tried to do, in providing an analysis of the specific and general claims of Christian witness, is to show how a nonpatriarchal and nonimperialistic interpretation of Christian witness and life is not only possible but warranted by the sources of Christian tradition and by more general arguments about the nature of reality and adequate human responses to it.

Further, to understand that the Christian witness of faith makes claims about the meaning of the nature of reality and of human response to it, and to try to set out what those claims are, opens venues of understanding and communication for those who do not consider themselves adherents of Christianity. In particular, it opens points of entry for persons of other religious traditions. To say: "Jesus is the Christ" could well cut off all understanding if it is made as a claim that one must take or leave without further ado. If one attempts seriously and critically to portray for another the view of reality and of ultimate reality or God that is implied by such a claim, several dimensions of interaction are opened. What is the nature of reality? What, if anything, in reality might be named as ultimate? Why do some name that ultimate reality "God"? How do others name what is ultimate in reality and why do they name it thus? What does this ultimate reality have to do with me? How does ultimate reality relate to the rest of the universe? These are all questions that ought to be opened by christological confession, not closed by it.

Likewise, multiple questions are opened by discussions of goodness and beauty. In what particular activities ought we to engage in order adequately to live out response to the God Christians find through Jesus? How do others live in response to other concepts of ultimate reality? Are there shared principles for action or values to be espoused that might arise from differing views of reality? How do the present contexts in

142

which we find ourselves provide shared questions and issues that must be addressed? Regardless of how motivations in ultimate reality for activity might be articulated, are there overlapping areas of activity that can be agreed upon across religious lines? What, beyond meeting survival needs, conduces to fullness of human life? Why and how does the view of reality presented make an impact on me? Why do human beings seek more from life than mere continued existence, as important as that is? How does nonhuman existence provide value? Does it provide merely instrumental value for human beings, or does it have value in and for itself or for some view of the whole of reality? Again, christological claims could and should open such discussion rather than close it. Christians need to begin seriously to see that the fullness of life they find fostered and espoused by the Christian tradition is not the province only of Christians.

Christian Claims alongside Other Claims

Are the values of truth, goodness, and beauty arrived at here through the Christian context also values that are espoused by other religious traditions? No claims have been made here that all religious traditions make the same claims about the nature of reality or about how human beings ought to live in response. The aims of this study have been more restricted. It has sought only to analyze or critically examine the claims made by Christians. It has argued that the Christian tradition seeks to provide answers to human questions about the meaning of the nature of reality and how we ought to respond that can be argued to be worthy of belief, action, and enjoyment. We have also argued that in the Christian tradition Jesus as the Christ re-presents or embodies rather than constitutes what is worthy of belief, action, and enjoyment. That is, we have argued that truth, goodness, and beauty are universal values, implicit in but accessible not only through the Christian symbol system and not only to Christians.

There may be other ways to construe the claims of religious traditions than through the concepts of truth, goodness, and beauty. Other patterns of organization and relation of general ideas may be suggested by other religious traditions. It would take steps in interreligious discussion beyond the scope of this book to see how the general claims made by the Christian witness of faith can be brought into relationship with general claims from other religious traditions.

Through its particularity, the Christian tradition embodies or re-presents the universal in the concrete. When we begin to analyze our experience, to reflect upon it, we recognize its particularities and the way in which our contexts inform our interpretations. But to begin our reflection with the particular is not necessarily to end there. When, in the past, analysis jumped too soon to false universals, much of the particularity of many lives was simply ignored or passed over. If we spend all our energy on pointing to particularities, to differences, we risk losing sight of the possibilities for commonality and interconnection.

When we begin to ask just what it is that is being claimed in and through particular Christian symbols, we come to more general claims that provide entry points for understanding for those who do not share the symbol system. Consensus and understanding are not the same thing. One can understand the claims another is making, one can understand the arguments that support those claims, one can even enter at least a certain distance into the experience of the one who makes the claims; yet one may, in the end, reject some or all of the claims being made because one can adduce arguments that tell against the claims in question. Each claim requires separate assessment. Understanding takes place on many levels. Argument and counterargument find many points of entry. Agreement on the implications of some religious claims may not necessarily lead to agreement on others.

Religious traditions are not simple but complex. There is no one simple way or method to see if religious traditions are making equivalent or roughly equivalent claims. Scholars of individual traditions are often disputing among themselves as to the central claims of any given tradition. Such difficulties do not absolve one of the responsibility for taking scholarly positions; they serve only, one hopes, to make one more modest in thinking about what one has accomplished.

I have argued that one both can and should understand the Christian witness of faith as one that sanctions neither imperialism nor patriarchy. The need for such an argument arises at all because serious questions have been raised by feminists and by those who question any a priori assumptions about the superiority of Christianity. Further, I have sought to show that by analyzing the Christian witness of faith one comes to a set of general claims that might well open doors to better understanding across religious lines and might well provide, for feminists who are not in the Christian tradition, points of entry into understanding why some feminists remain in the Christian tradition.

Admittedly, the Christian tradition takes many historical and cultural forms and has many interpreters. The interpretation set forth here seeks to be an adequate presentation of the Christian witness of faith, which is, at the same time, by virtue of the universal claims of this faith tradition, credible according to generally accessible arguments. One does not have to abandon all specific religious claims in order to take another's position seriously. What one does have to do, however, is constantly to be examining one's own position to see whether its specifics as articulated and lived out foster or impede its general claims.

When one claims "Jesus is the Christ," when one tells the stories of Jesus, when one sings the hymns of the church, when one takes part in the Eucharist, one is enacting one's witness of faith. The task of the theologian, and indeed, to a certain extent of all reflective Christians, is to reflect critically on whether such claims and activities are appropriately part of the Christian tradition and whether they can be sustained in light of questions about the sorts of claims that are being made. Here it is argued that the Christian witness of faith tells the truth about the nature of reality, sanctions activities that advance moral good, and fosters the satisfaction of experience for all creatures and for God. Such a position does *not* require as a corollary that if the Christian tradition does as is claimed here, no other tradition can do the same.

Like most projects that engage us over long periods of time, this book is not merely an intellectual exercise, but a contribution to a personal quest. I struggle with my own identity as a Christian and a feminist in a world where some forms of Christianity have been responsible for or complicitous in oppressing non-Christians, the poor, women, and the earth. But the same symbols that oppress have also had enormous liberating power. One purpose of this book has been to explore how those liberating possibilities might be realized by showing how certain kinds of Christian identity can provide for one possibility of human flourishing while living in integrity with all one's human and nonhuman neighbors in a world where there are many religious options. The Christian identity that I seek is one that recognizes the interconnectedness of all that is and fosters partnership among all creatures in working toward integrity for all who share the world.

To be human at the end of the millennium is to take on a complex identity and set of commitments. To be a reflective ' human being is to seek to understand and to be able to articulate the context from which one makes commitments and the reasons for the commitments one makes. This book has sought to be one contribution to the ongoing process of naming and understanding oneself and the others with whom one shares the world.

Notes

Chapter 1

1. See, e.g., Gavin D'Costa, *Theology and Religious Pluralism: The Challenge of Other Religions* (Oxford: Basil Blackwell, 1986); and Alan Race, *Christians and Religious Pluralism* (Maryknoll, N.Y.: Orbis, 1982).

2. See, e.g., D'Costa, *Theology and Religious Pluralism,* 80-116; and Race, *Christians and Religious Pluralism,* 38-69.

3. See, e.g., D'Costa, *Theology and Religious Pluralism,* 22-31; and Race, *Christians and Religious Pluralism,* 70-105.

4. John Cobb, "Christian Witness in a Plural World," in *The Experience of Religious Diversity,* ed. John Hick and Hasan Askari (Brookfield, Vt.: Gower, 1985), 146.

5. See, e.g., Christoph Schwöbel, "Particularity, Universality and the Religions," in *Christian Uniqueness Reconsidered: The Myth of a Pluralistic Theology of Religions,* ed. Gavin D'Costa (Maryknoll, N.Y.: Orbis, 1990), 30-46.

6. John Hick, *God Has Many Names* (Philadelphia: Westminster, 1980), 24.

7. More will be said about each of these options throughout the book.

8. Schubert M. Ogden, *Is There Only One True Religion or Are There Many?* (Dallas: Southern Methodist Univ. Press, 1992).

9. See Michel Foucault, *The Archaeology of Knowledge,* trans. A. M. Sheridan Smith (London: Tavistock, 1972).

10. Luce Irigaray, *Sexes and Genealogies,* trans. Gillian C. Gill (New York: Columbia Univ. Press, 1993), 140, 194-95.

Chapter 2

1. See, e.g., Riffat Hassan, "Muslim Women and Post-Patriarchal Islam," and Rita Gross, "Buddhism after Patriarchy?" in Paula M. Cooey, William R. Eakin, and Jay B. McDaniel, eds., *After Patriarchy: Feminist Transformation of the World Religions* (Maryknoll, N.Y.: Orbis, 1991), 39-64, 65-86; and Rita Gross, *Buddhism after Patriarchy: A Feminist History,*

Analysis and Reconstruction of Buddhism (Albany: State Univ. of New York Press, 1993).

2. Examples are Daphne Hampson, *Theology and Feminism* (Cambridge: Basil Blackwell, 1990), and Mary Daly, *Beyond God the Father: Toward a Philosophy of Women's Liberation* (Boston: Beacon, 1973).

3. See, e.g., Eleanor McLaughlin, "The Christian Past: Does It Hold a Future for Women?" in Carol P. Christ and Judith Plaskow, eds., *Womanspirit Rising: A Feminist Reader in Religion* (New York: Harper and Row, 1979), and Elizabeth A. Johnson, *She Who Is: The Mystery of God in Feminist Theological Discourse* (New York: Crossroad, 1992).

4. See Sallie McFague, *Models of God: Theology for an Ecological, Nuclear Age* (Philadelphia: Fortress, 1987), and *The Body of God: An Ecological Theology* (Minneapolis: Fortress, 1993).

5. See Rosemary Radford Ruether, *New Woman New Earth: Sexist Ideologies and Human Liberation* (New York: Seabury, 1975), and *Sexism and God-Talk: Toward a Feminist Theology* (Boston: Beacon, 1983).

6. See Daly, *Beyond God the Father.* See also Jeanne Becher, ed., *Women, Religion and Sexuality: Studies on the Impact of Religious Teachings on Women* (Geneva: WCC Publications, 1990).

7. Judith Plaskow, *Standing Again at Sinai: Judaism from a Feminist Perspective* (San Francisco: Harper and Row, 1990).

8. Rita Gross, "Female God Language in a Jewish Context," in Christ and Plaskow, eds., *Womanspirit Rising,* 172.

9. See, e.g., Rita Gross, "Steps toward Feminine Imagery of Deity in Jewish Theology," in Susannah Heschel, ed., *On Being a Jewish Feminist: A Reader* (New York: Schocken, 1983), 234-47; and Plaskow, *Standing Again at Sinai,* 121-69.

10. Laura Geller, "Reactions to a Woman Rabbi," in Heschel, ed., *On Being a Jewish Feminist,* 210-13.

11. Deborah E. Lipstadt, "And Deborah Made Ten," in Heschel, ed., *On Being a Jewish Feminist,* 207-9.

12. See Rachel Biale, *Women and Jewish Law* (New York: Schocken, 1984).

13. Plaskow, *Standing Again at Sinai,* 28.

14. Ibid., 185.

15. Ibid., 170-210; see also Blu Greenberg, "Female Sexuality and Bodily Functions in the Jewish Tradition"; and Pnina Navè Levinson, "Women and Sexuality: Traditions and Progress," in Becher, ed., *Women, Religion and Sexuality,* 1-44, 45-63.

16. Plaskow, *Standing Again at Sinai,* 194-97.

17. For example, see Jane I. Smith, "Islam," in Arvind Sharma, ed., *Women in World Religions* (New York: State Univ. of New York Press, 1987), 235-50.

18. Riffat Hassan, "Muslim Women and Post-Patriarchal Islam," in Cooey, Eakin, and McDaniel, eds., *After Patriarchy,* 60.

19. See ibid., 55; and Smith, "Islam," in Sharma, ed., *Women in World Religions,* 236.

Christ in a Post-Christian World

20. Azizah al-Hibri, "A Study of Islamic Herstory," in Azizah al-Hibri, ed., *Women and Islam* (Willowdale, Ont.: Pergamon Press, 1982), 218.

21. Hassan, "Muslim Women and Post-Patriarchal Islam," in Cooey, Eakin, and McDaniel, eds., *After Patriarchy*, 57.

22. See Annemarie Schimmel, "Women in Mystical Islam," in al-Hibri, ed., *Women and Islam*, 145; and Smith, "Islam," in Sharma, ed., *Women in World Religions*, 243.

23. See, e.g., Fatima Mernissi, "Virginity and Patriarchy," in al-Hibri, ed., *Women and Islam*, 183-91.

24. See Nawal el Saadawi, "Woman and Islam," in al-Hibri, ed., *Women and Islam*, 202; and Smith, "Islam," in Sharma, ed., *Women in World Religions*, 240.

25. Lina Gupta, "Kali, the Savior," in Cooey, Eakin, and McDaniel, eds., *After Patriarchy*, 15-38.

26. Katherine K. Young, "Women in Hinduism," in Sharma, ed., *Women in World Religions*, 59-103.

27. See Doranne Jacobson, "Golden Handprints and Red-Painted Feet: Hindu Childbirth Rituals in Central India"; Susan S. Wadley, "Hindu Women's Family and Household Rites in a North Indian Village"; James M. Freeman, "The Ladies of Lord Krishna: Rituals of Middle-Aged Women in Eastern India"; in Nancy A. Falk and Rita M. Gross, eds., *Unspoken Worlds: Women's Religious Lives in Non-Western Cultures* (San Francisco: Harper and Row, 1980), 73-93, 94-109, and 110-26.

28. See Katherine K. Young, "Women in Hinduism," in Arvind Sharma, ed., *Today's Woman in World Religions* (Albany: State Univ. of New York Press, 1994), 130.

29. Young, "Hinduism," in Sharma, ed., *Women in World Religions*, 65.

30. Vasudha Narayanan, "Hindu Perceptions of Auspiciousness and Sexuality," in Becher, ed., *Women, Religion and Sexuality*, 64-92.

31. Gross, *Buddhism after Patriarchy*, 137.

32. Ibid., 138-39.

33. Nancy J. Barnes, "Women in Buddhism," in Sharma, ed., *Today's Woman*, 159.

34. Gross, *Buddhism after Patriarchy*, 105ff.

35. See Margot Adler, *Drawing Down the Moon: Witches, Druids, Goddess-Worshippers, and Other Pagans in America Today* (Boston: Beacon, 1986); and Charlene Spretnak, ed., *The Politics of Women's Spirituality: Essays on the Rise of Spiritual Power within the Feminist Movement* (New York: Anchor, 1982).

36. See Maura O'Neill, *Women Speaking, Women Listening: Women in Interreligious Dialogue* (Maryknoll, N.Y.: Orbis, 1990); Rosemary Radford Ruether, "Feminism and Jewish-Christian Dialogue: Particularism and Universalism in the Search for Religious Truth," in John Hick and Paul Knitter, eds., *The Myth of Christian Uniqueness: Toward a Pluralistic Theology of Religions* (Maryknoll, N.Y.: Orbis, 1987), 137-48; Marjorie Hewitt Suchocki, "In Search of Justice: Religious Pluralism from a Feminist Perspective," in Hick and Knitter, eds., *The Myth of Christian Uniqueness*, 149-61.

Notes

37. Suchocki, "In Search of Justice," in Hick and Knitter, eds., *The Myth of Christian Uniqueness,* 154.

38. See Seyla Benhabib, *Situating the Self: Gender, Community and Postmodernism in Contemporary Ethics* (Cambridge: Polity, 1992).

39. This term is regularly used to speak of an approach that questions the presuppositions and power dynamics underlying a given text or claim. See, e.g., Elisabeth Schüssler Fiorenza, *Bread Not Stone: The Challenge of Feminist Biblical Interpretation* (Boston: Beacon, 1984), 16ff.

40. Paul F. Knitter, *No Other Name? A Critical Survey of Christian Attitudes toward the World Religions* (Maryknoll, N.Y.: Orbis, 1985), 171.

41. John Hick, "Religious Pluralism and Absolute Claims," in Leroy Rouner, ed., *Religious Pluralism* (Notre Dame, Ind.: Univ. of Notre Dame Press, 1984), 200.

42. Rosemary Radford Ruether, *To Change the World: Christology and Cultural Criticism* (New York: Crossroad, 1981), 31.

43. Ibid., 42.

44. Knitter, *No Other Name,* 173.

45. Peter Slater, *The Dynamics of Religion: Meaning and Change in Religious Traditions* (San Francisco: Harper and Row, 1978), 15.

46. See ibid., 28.

47. Tom Driver, *Christ in a Changing World* (New York: Crossroad, 1981); Raimundo Panikkar, "Religious Pluralism: The Metaphysical Challenge," in Rouner, ed., *Religious Pluralism,* 97-115.

48. See, e.g., Sheila Greeve Davaney, "Problems with Feminist Theory: Historicity and the Search for Sure Foundations," in Paula Cooey, Sharon Farmer, and Mary Ellen Ross, eds., *Embodied Love: Sensuality and Relationship as Feminist Values* (San Francisco: Harper and Row, 1983), 79-96.

49. Suchocki, "In Search of Justice," in Hick and Knitter, eds., *The Myth of Christian Uniqueness,* 150.

Chapter 3

1. John Hick, *God Has Many Names* (Philadelphia: Westminster, 1980), 117.

2. Ibid., 56.

3. Ibid., 74.

4. Ibid., 75.

5. See John Hick, "On Grading Religions," *Religious Studies* 17 (1981), 451-67.

6. Hick, *God Has Many Names,* 71.

7. Rosemary Radford Ruether, "Feminism and Jewish-Christian Dialogue: Particularism and Universalism in the Search for Religious Truth," in John Hick and Paul F. Knitter, eds., *The Myth of Christian Uniqueness: Toward a Pluralistic Theology of Religions* (Maryknoll, N.Y.: Orbis, 1987), 141.

8. Ibid., 146.

9. Rosemary Radford Ruether, *Sexism and God-Talk: Toward a*

Feminist Theology (Boston: Beacon, 1983), 138.

10. Paul F. Knitter, *No Other Name? A Critical Survey of Christian Attitudes toward the World Religions* (Maryknoll, N.Y.: Orbis, 1985), 173.

11. Knitter, *No Other Name?* 172.

12. Paul F. Knitter, "Interreligious Dialogue: What? Why? How?" in Leonard Swidler, John Cobb, Paul F. Knitter, and Monica K. Hellwig, *Death or Dialogue? From the Age of Monologue to the Age of Dialogue* (London: SCM, 1990), 37.

13. Knitter, "Interreligious Dialogue," in Swidler, Cobb, Knitter, and Hellwig, *Death or Dialogue?* 41.

14. J. A. Dinoia, *The Diversity of Religions: A Christian Perspective* (Washington, D.C.: Catholic Univ. of America, 1992), 49-53.

15. Raimundo Panikkar, "The Jordan, the Tiber and the Ganges: Three Kairological Moments of Christic Self-Consciousness," in Hick and Knitter, eds., *The Myth of Christian Uniqueness,* 109.

16. Ibid., 109.

17. Alan Race, *Christians and Religious Pluralism: Patterns in the Christian Theology of Religions* (Maryknoll, N.Y.: Orbis, 1982), 135-36.

18. Christoph Schwöbel, "Particularity, Universality and the Religions: Toward a Christian Theology of Religions," in Gavin D'Costa, ed., *Christian Uniqueness Reconsidered: The Myth of a Pluralistic Theology of Religions* (Maryknoll, N.Y.: Orbis, 1990), 33.

19. Daphne Hampson, *Theology and Feminism* (Oxford: Basil Blackwell, 1990), 76.

20. See, e.g., Willi Marxsen, *Jesus and the Church: The Beginnings of Christianity,* trans. Philip E. Devenish (Philadelphia: Trinity Press International, 1992), 16-25.

21. See, e.g., Marinus de Jonge, *Christology in Context: The Earliest Christian Response to Jesus* (Philadelphia: Westminster, 1988), 11.

22. Ibid., 11, 203-11.

23. Ibid., 214.

24. Ibid., 83.

25. Ibid., 85.

26. Ibid., 158.

27. John Dominic Crossan, *The Historical Jesus: The Life of a Jewish Mediterranean Peasant* (San Francisco: HarperCollins, 1991), 287.

28. Ibid., 292.

29. Ibid., 298.

30. Ibid.

31. Ibid., 422.

32. Ibid., xi.

33. Ibid., xiii-xxvi.

34. Karl Rahner, *Foundations of Christian Faith: An Introduction to the Idea of Christianity,* trans. William V. Dych (New York: Crossroad, 1978), 142.

35. Schubert M. Ogden, *The Point of Christology* (San Francisco: Harper and Row 1982), 29-30.

Notes

36. Ibid., 34-35.

37. Friedrich Schleiermacher, *The Christian Faith,* ed. H. R. Mackintosh and J. S. Stewart (Edinburgh: T. & T. Clark, 1928), 5ff.

38. See, e.g., Charles Hartshorne, *Creative Synthesis and Philosophic Method* (LaSalle, Ill.: Open Court, 1970), 303.

39. For use of this term, see Schubert M. Ogden, *Is There One True Religion or Are There Many?* (Dallas: Southern Methodist Univ. Press, 1992), 82ff.

40. See, e.g., de Jonge, *Christology in Context,* 92-93.

41. See Pamela Dickey Young, *Feminist Theology/Christian Theology: In Search of Method* (Minneapolis: Fortress, 1990), 80-90.

42. Krister Stendahl, "Notes for Three Bible Studies," in Gerald H. Anderson and Thomas F. Stransky, eds., *Christ's Lordship and Religious Pluralism* (Maryknoll, N.Y.: Orbis, 1981), 14.

43. Crossan, *The Historical Jesus,* xiv.

44. Ogden, *Is There One True Religion or Are There Many?* 92.

45. Odgen, *The Point of Christology,* 78.

46. Ibid., 121-22.

47. S. J. Samartha, *One Christ—Many Religions: Toward a Revised Christology* (Maryknoll, N.Y.: Orbis, 1991), 152.

48. Leonard Swidler, *After the Absolute: The Dialogical Future of Religious Reflection* (Minneapolis: Fortress, 1990), 203.

49. Leonard Swidler, "A Dialogue on Dialogue," in Swidler, Cobb, Knitter, and Hellwig, *Death or Dialogue?* 74.

50. Samartha, *One Christ—Many Religions,* 132-34.

51. Ibid., 115.

52. John B. Cobb, Jr., "The Meaning of Pluralism for Christian Self-Understanding," in Leroy S. Rouner, ed., *Religious Pluralism* (Notre Dame, Ind.: Univ. of Notre Dame Press, 1984), 177.

53. Caroline Walker Bynum, "Introduction: The Complexity of Symbols," in Caroline Walker Bynum, Stevan Harrell, and Paula Richman, eds., *Gender and Religion: On the Complexity of Symbols* (Boston: Beacon, 1986), 2-5.

54. See, e.g., Katherine K. Young, "Introduction," and "Hinduism," in Arvind Sharma, ed., *Women in World Religions* (Albany: State Univ. of New York Press, 1987), 10-36, 59-104.

55. Elizabeth A. Johnson, *She Who Is: The Mystery of God in Feminist Theological Discourse* (New York: Crossroad, 1992), 150-69.

56. Mircea Eliade, *Images and Symbols: Studies in Religious Symbolism,* trans. Philip Mairet (London: Harwell, 1961), 17.

57. Paul Ricoeur, "Toward a Hermeneutic of the Idea of Revelation," in idem, *Essays on Biblical Interpretation,* ed. and introduced by Lewis Mudge (Philadelphia: Fortress, 1980), 101.

Chapter 4

1. For one accounting of the earliest gospel material, see John Dominic Crossan, *The Historical Jesus: The Life of a Mediterranean Jewish Peasant*

(San Francisco: HarperCollins, 1991), xiii-xxvi. In this material, God is most often inferred from parable and metaphor rather than directly described. Some of the early texts include: "The kingdom of God is already among you." "Consider the ravens: they neither sow nor reap, they have neither storehouse nor barn, and yet God feeds them." "The Kingdom is like a shepherd who had a hundred sheep. He left the ninety-nine and looked for that one until he found it." "How much more will your Father who is in heaven give good things to those who ask him!" "Are not five sparrows sold for two pennies? And not one of them is forgotten before God." This material also contains the parables of the laborers in the vineyard, the lost coin, and the prodigal son.

2. Keith Ward, "Truth and the Diversity of Religions," *Religious Studies* 26 (1990): 16.

3. Gordon D. Kaufman, "Religious Diversity, Historical Consciousness, and Christian Theology," in John Hick and Paul F. Knitter, eds., *The Myth of Christian Uniqueness: Toward a Pluralistic Theology of Religions* (Maryknoll, N.Y.: Orbis, 1987), 9, 14.

4. Ibid., 12-13.

5. Ibid., 11.

6. Paul F. Knitter, *No Other Name? A Critical Survey of Christian Attitudes toward the World Religions* (Maryknoll, N.Y.: Orbis, 1989), 219.

7. Ibid., 220.

8. Ibid., 231.

9. Ibid., 220.

10. Leonard Swidler, *After the Absolute: The Dialogical Future of Religious Reflection* (Minneapolis: Fortress, 1990), 13.

11. Masao Abe, "'There Is No Common Denominator for World Religions': The Positive Meaning of This Negative Statement," *Journal of Ecumenical Studies* 26 (1989): 78.

12. Masao Abe, "A Dynamic Unity in Religious Pluralism: A Proposal from the *Buddhist* Point of View," in John Hick and Hasan Askari, eds., *The Experience of Religious Diversity* (Aldershot, U.K.: Gower, 1985), 189-90.

13. See, e.g., Raimundo Panikkar, "Religious Pluralism: The Metaphysical Challenge," in Leroy Rouner, ed., *Religious Pluralism* (Notre Dame, Ind.: Univ. of Notre Dame Press, 1984), 98.

14. Raimundo Panikkar, "The Jordan, the Tiber and the Ganges: Three Kairological Moments of Christic Self-Consciousness," in Hick and Knitter, eds., *The Myth of Christian Uniqueness,* 109.

15. Raimundo Panikkar, "Religious Pluralism," 99-100.

16. Langdon Gilkey, "Plurality and Its Theological Implications," in Hick and Knitter, eds., *Myth of Christian Uniqueness,* 49.

17. Ibid., 47.

18. Ibid., 43.

19. Wilfred Cantwell Smith, *Towards a World Theology: Faith and the Comparative History of Religion* (Philadelphia: Westminster, 1981), 97.

20. Ibid.

21. Wilfred Cantwell Smith, "Idolatry: In Comparative Perspective," in

Notes

Hick and Knitter, eds., *The Myth of Christian Uniqueness*, 65.

22. Roger Trigg, "Religion and the Threat of Relativism," *Religious Studies* 19 (1983): 298-99.

23. Gregory Baum, "Radical Pluralism and Liberation Theology," in Werner G. Jeanrond and Jennifer L. Rike, eds., *Radical Pluralism and Truth: David Tracy and the Hermeneutics of Religion* (New York: Crossroad), 15.

24. John Hick, *An Interpretation of Religion: Human Responses to the Transcendent* (Basingstoke, U.K.: Macmillan, 1989), 248-49.

25. John Hick, *God Has Many Names* (Philadelphia: Westminster, 1980), 24.

26. John Hick, "Religious Pluralism and Absolute Claims," in Rouner, ed., *Religious Pluralism*, 194.

27. Timothy R. Stinnett, "John Hick's Pluralistic Theory of Religion," *Journal of Religion* 70 (1990), 584. Stinnett's article is a good critical discussion of some of the presuppositions and implications of Hick's pluralistic hypothesis.

28. John Hick, "On Grading Religions," *Religious Studies* 17 (1981), 466-67.

29. Alfred North Whitehead, *Modes of Thought* (New York: Free Press, 1938), 110.

30. Ibid.

31. Ibid.

32. Ibid., 116.

33. See, e.g., Mary E. Hunt, *Fierce Tenderness: A Feminist Theology of Friendship* (New York: Crossroad, 1991); see also the section on "Self in Relation" in Judith Plaskow and Carol Christ, eds., *Weaving the Visions: New Patterns in Feminist Spirituality* (San Francisco: Harper and Row, 1989), 171-266.

34. Whitehead, *Modes of Thought*, 120.

35. See John B. Cobb, Jr., "Dialogue," in Leonard Swidler, John B. Cobb, Jr., Paul F. Knitter, and Monica K. Hellwig, *Death or Dialogue? From the Age of Monologue to the Age of Dialogue* (London: SCM, 1990), 6; and "Christian Witness in a Plural World," in Hick and Askari, eds., *The Experience of Religious Diversity*, 157.

36. See, e.g., Charles Hartshorne, *Creative Synthesis and Philosophic Method* (LaSalle, Ill.: Open Court, 1970), 275-97.

37. See, e.g., Charles Hartshorne, *A Natural Theology for Our Time* (LaSalle, Ill.: Open Court, 1973), 29-65.

38. Hartshorne, *Creative Synthesis and Philosophic Method*, 232-33.

39. See, e.g., Sallie McFague, *Models of God: Theology for an Ecological, Nuclear Age* (Philadelphia: Fortress, 1987), and Charles Hartshorne, *A Natural Theology for Our Time*, 98ff.

40. See Sallie McFague, *The Body of God: An Ecological Theology* (Minneapolis: Fortress, 1993), 141-50.

41. Anna Case-Winters, *God's Power: Traditional Understandings and Contemporary Challenges* (Louisville: Westminster/John Knox, 1990).

42. This argument is found in most of the essays in Alvin Kimel, ed., *Speaking the Christian God: The Holy Trinity and the Challenge of Feminism* (Grand Rapids, Mich.: Wm. B. Eerdmans, 1992).

43. Elizabeth A. Johnson, *She Who Is: The Mystery of God in Feminist Discourse* (New York: Crossroad, 1992), 80-81. This book is an excellent feminist discussion of the question of God in Christian theology.

44. Two recent books that provide a variety of useful and usable images and metaphors for God are Elizabeth A. Johnson's *She Who Is* and Sallie McFague's *The Body of God*.

45. Sheila Greeve Davaney, "Problems with Feminist Theory: Historicity and the Search for Sure Foundations," in Paula M. Cooey, Sharon A. Farmer, and Mary Ellen Ross, eds., *Embodied Love: Sensuality and Relationship as Feminist Values* (San Francisco: Harper and Row, 1983), 93.

46. Carol Christ, "Embodied Thinking: Reflections on Feminist Theological Method," *Journal of Feminist Studies in Religion* 5 (1989), 13.

Chapter 5

1. John Dominic Crossan, *The Historical Jesus: The Life of a Mediterranean Jewish Peasant* (San Francisco: HarperCollins, 1991), 423.

2. See, e.g., Victor Paul Furnish, *The Moral Teaching of Paul: Selected Issues,* 2nd ed. (Nashville: Abingdon, 1985).

3. John Hick, "On Grading Religions," *Religious Studies* 17 (1981), 466-67.

4. Paul F. Knitter, *No Other Name? A Critical Survey of Christian Attitudes toward the World Religions* (Maryknoll, N.Y.: Orbis, 1985), 231.

5. Paul F. Knitter, "Toward a Liberation Theology of Religions," in John Hick and Paul F. Knitter, eds., *The Myth of Christian Uniqueness: Toward a Pluralistic Theology of Religions* (Maryknoll, N.Y.: Orbis, 1987), 189.

6. Paul F. Knitter, "Interreligious Dialogue: What? Why? How?" in Leonard Swidler, John B. Cobb, Jr., Paul F. Knitter, and Monica Hellwig, *Death or Dialogue? From the Age of Monologue to the Age of Dialogue* (London: SCM, 1990), 30.

7. Knitter, "Toward a Liberation Theology of Religions," 189, 190.

8. Knitter, "Interreligious Dialogue," 33.

9. Marjorie Suchocki, "In Search of Justice: Religious Pluralism from a Feminist Perspective," in Hick and Knitter, eds., *The Myth of Christian Uniqueness*, 154.

10. Ibid.

11. Ibid.

12. Ibid., 155.

13. Ibid., 159.

14. Ibid.

15. See Elizabeth V. Spelman, *Inessential Woman: Problems of Exclusion in Feminist Thought* (Boston: Beacon, 1988), for a very helpful discussion of how categories meant to be inclusive often function exclusively.

16. See, e.g., Edith Wyschogrod, *Saints and Postmodernism: Revisioning*

Moral Philosophy (Chicago: University of Chicago Press, 1990).

17. See Seyla Benhabib, *Situating the Self: Gender, Community and Postmodernism in Contemporary Ethics* (Cambridge: Polity Press, 1992).

18. Ibid., 8.

19. Ibid., 4.

20. Suchocki, "In Search of Justice," 154.

21. Nellie McClung, *In Times like These* (Toronto: Univ. of Toronto Press, 1972), 79.

Chapter 6

1. See, e.g., Rosemary Radford Ruether, *Sexism and God-Talk: Toward a Feminist Theology* (Boston: Beacon, 1983), 72ff.

2. Charles Hartshorne, *Creative Synthesis and Philosophic Method* (LaSalle, Ill.: Open Court, 1970), 303.

3. Lorraine Code, *What Can She Know? Feminist Theory and the Construction of Knowledge* (Ithaca, N.Y.: Cornell University Press, 1991), 47.

4. Hartshorne, *Creative Synthesis and Philosophic Method,* 304.

5. Ibid., 307.

6. Ibid., 304.

7. Charles Hartshorne, *Man's Vision of God and the Logic of Theism* (Hamden, Conn.: Archon, 1964), 214.

8. Charles Hartshorne, "A Dual Theory of Theological Analogy," *American Journal of Theology and Philosophy* 10 (1989): 174-75.

9. Frank Burch Brown, *Religious Aesthetics: A Theological Study of Making and Meaning* (Basingstoke, U.K.: Macmillan, 1990), 114.

10. Alice Walker, *The Color Purple* (New York: Washington Square Press, 1982), 178-79.

11. Brown, *Religious Aesthetics,* 179.

12. Elisabeth Schüssler Fiorenza, "Feminist Spirituality, Christian Identity, and Catholic Vision," in Carol Christ and Judith Plaskow, eds., *Womanspirit Rising: A Feminist Reader in Religion* (San Francisco: Harper and Row, 1979), 137.

13. See, e.g., Rosemary Radford Ruether, *Gaia and God: An Ecofeminist Theology of Earth Healing* (San Francisco: HarperCollins, 1992).

14. Audre Lorde, "Uses of the Erotic: The Erotic as Power," in Judith Plaskow and Carol P. Christ, eds., *Weaving the Visions: New Patterns in Feminist Spirituality* (San Francisco: Harper and Row, 1989), 209.

15. Lorde, "Uses of the Erotic," 211.

16. Ibid., 213.

17. Marilyn French, "Is There a Feminist Aesthetic?" *Hypatia* 5 (1990): 38.

18. Ibid., 41-42.

19. See, e.g., Clifford G. Hospital's account of being drawn into the experience of Hindu worship in a temple in Kerala in his "Christian Puja?" *Toronto Journal of Theology* 1 (Spring 1985): 80-92.

20. Hartshorne, *Creative Synthesis and Philosophic Method,* 303.

21. Brown, *Religious Aesthetics,* 145.

22. Ibid., 40.

23. Hartshorne, "A Dual Theory," 175.

Chapter 7

1. The United Church of Canada, *Record of Proceedings of the Thirty-Third General Council* (Toronto: United Church of Canada, 1990), 169-70.

2. United Church of Canada, *Record of Proceedings of the Thirty-Fourth General Council* (Toronto: United Church of Canada, 1992), 74-76.

3. Victoria, *Times-Colonist,* July 21, 1993.

4. Hugo Meynell, "The Conditions of Christian Uniqueness," *Journal of Ecumenical Studies* 26 (1989): 65.

Index

159